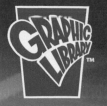

GRAPHIC LIBRARY

GRAPHIC SCIENCE

UNDERSTANDING PHOTOSYNTHESIS

WITH MAX AXIOM SUPER SCIENTIST

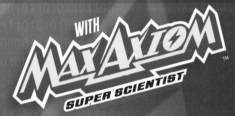

by by Liam O'Donnell | illustrated by Richard Dominguez and Charles Barnett III

Consultant:
Dr. Ronald Browne
Associate Professor of Elementary Education
Minnesota State University, Mankato

CAPSTONE PRESS
a capstone imprint

Graphic Library is published by Capstone Press,
1710 Roe Crest Drive, North Mankato, Minnesota 56003.
www.mycapstone.com

Library of Congress Cataloging-in-Publication Data is available on the Library of Congress website.
ISBN: 978-1-5435-2952-4 (library binding)
ISBN: 978-1-5435-2963-0 (paperback)
ISBN: 978-1-5435-2973-9 (eBook PDF)

Summary: In graphic novel format, follows the adventures of Max Axiom as he explains the science behind photosynthesis.

Art Director and Designer
Bob Lentz

Colorist
Michael Kelleher

Cover Artist
Tod Smith

Editor
Christopher L. Harbo

Photo Credits
Capstone Studio/Karon Dubke: 29

Printed in the United States 5576

TABLE OF CONTENTS

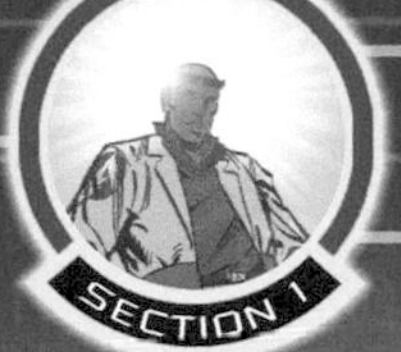
SECTION 1

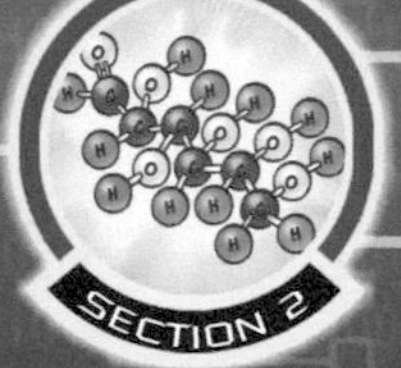
SECTION 2

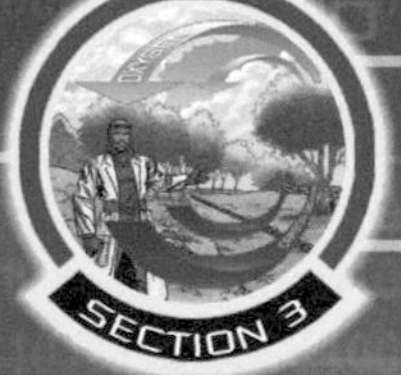
SECTION 3

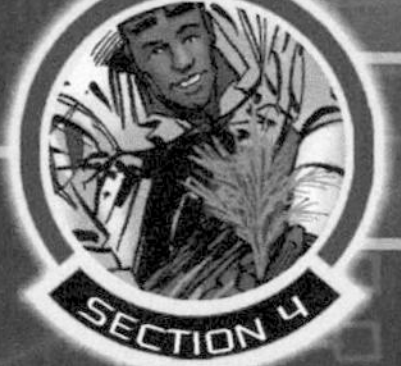
SECTION 4

SECTION 1 FOOD FROM THE SUN

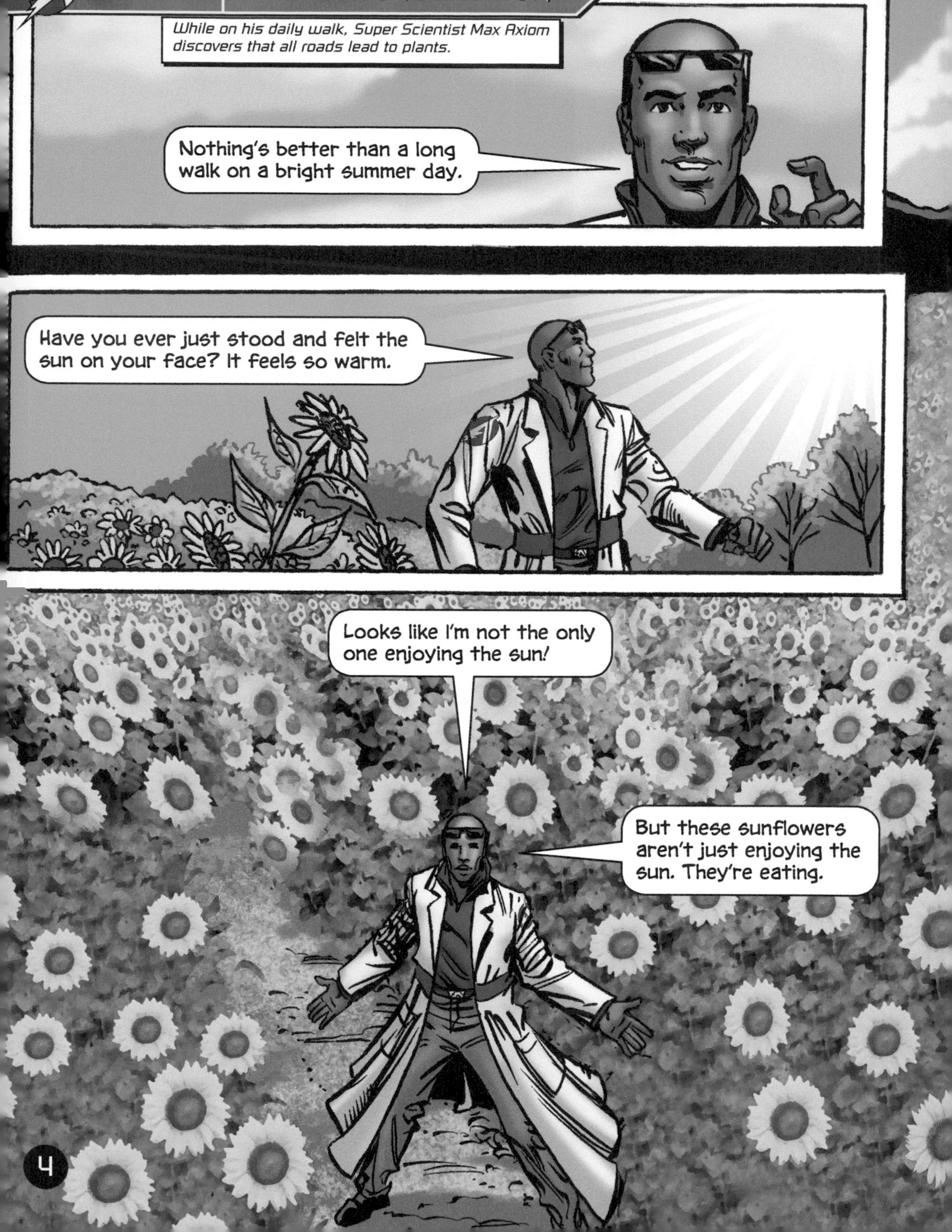

While on his daily walk, Super Scientist Max Axiom discovers that all roads lead to plants.
Nothing's better than a long walk on a bright summer day.
Have you ever just stood and felt the sun on your face? It feels so warm.
Looks like I'm not the only one enjoying the sun!
But these sunflowers aren't just enjoying the sun. They're eating.

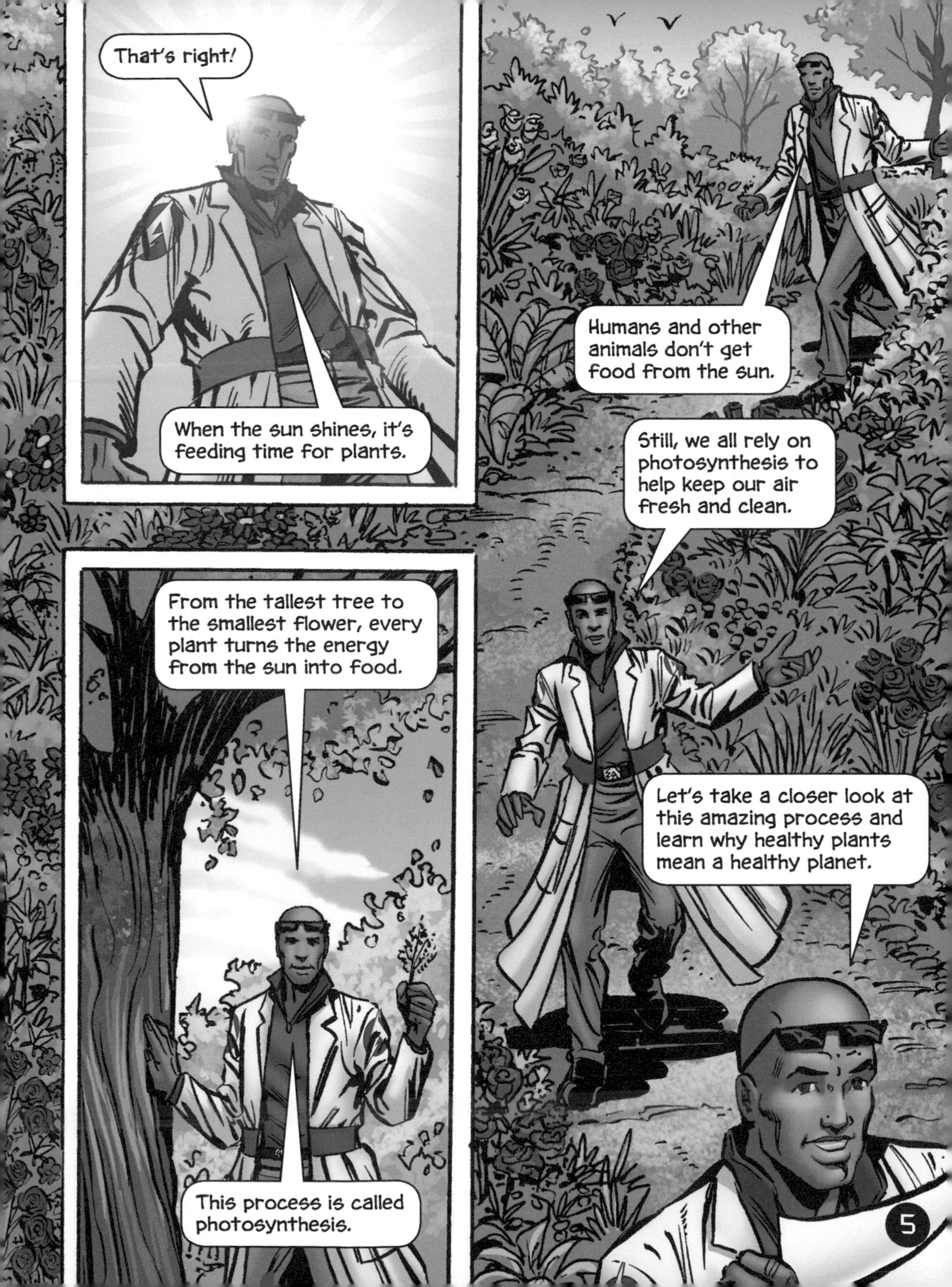

That's right!
When the sun shines, it's feeding time for plants.
From the tallest tree to the smallest flower, every plant turns the energy from the sun into food.
This process is called photosynthesis.
Humans and other animals don't get food from the sun.
Still, we all rely on photosynthesis to help keep our air fresh and clean.
Let's take a closer look at this amazing process and learn why healthy plants mean a healthy planet.

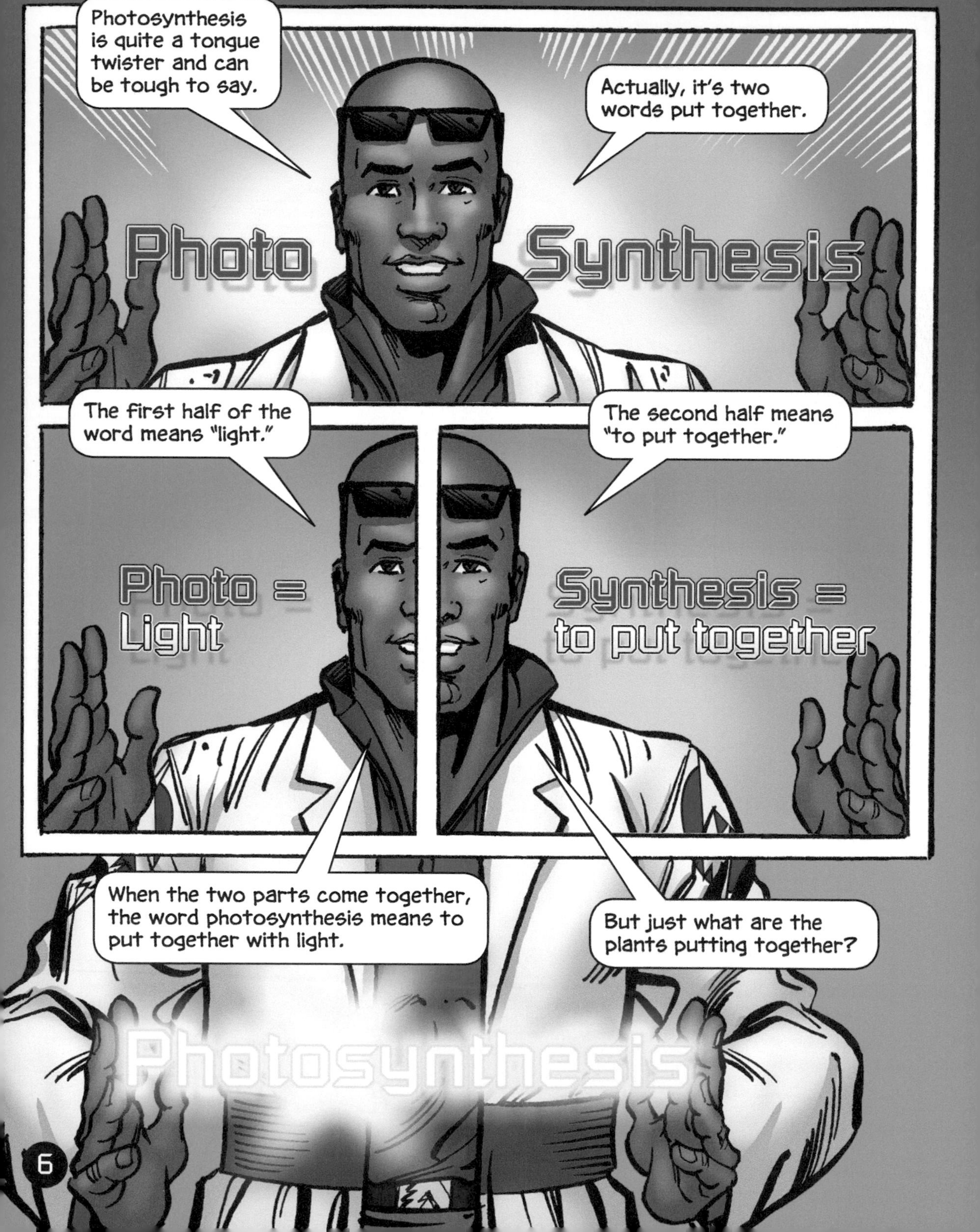
Photosynthesis is quite a tongue twister and can be tough to say.
Actually, it's two words put together.
Photo
Synthesis
The first half of the word means "light."
The second half means "to put together."
Photo = Light
Synthesis = to put together
When the two parts come together, the word photosynthesis means to put together with light.
But just what are the plants putting together?
Photosynthesis

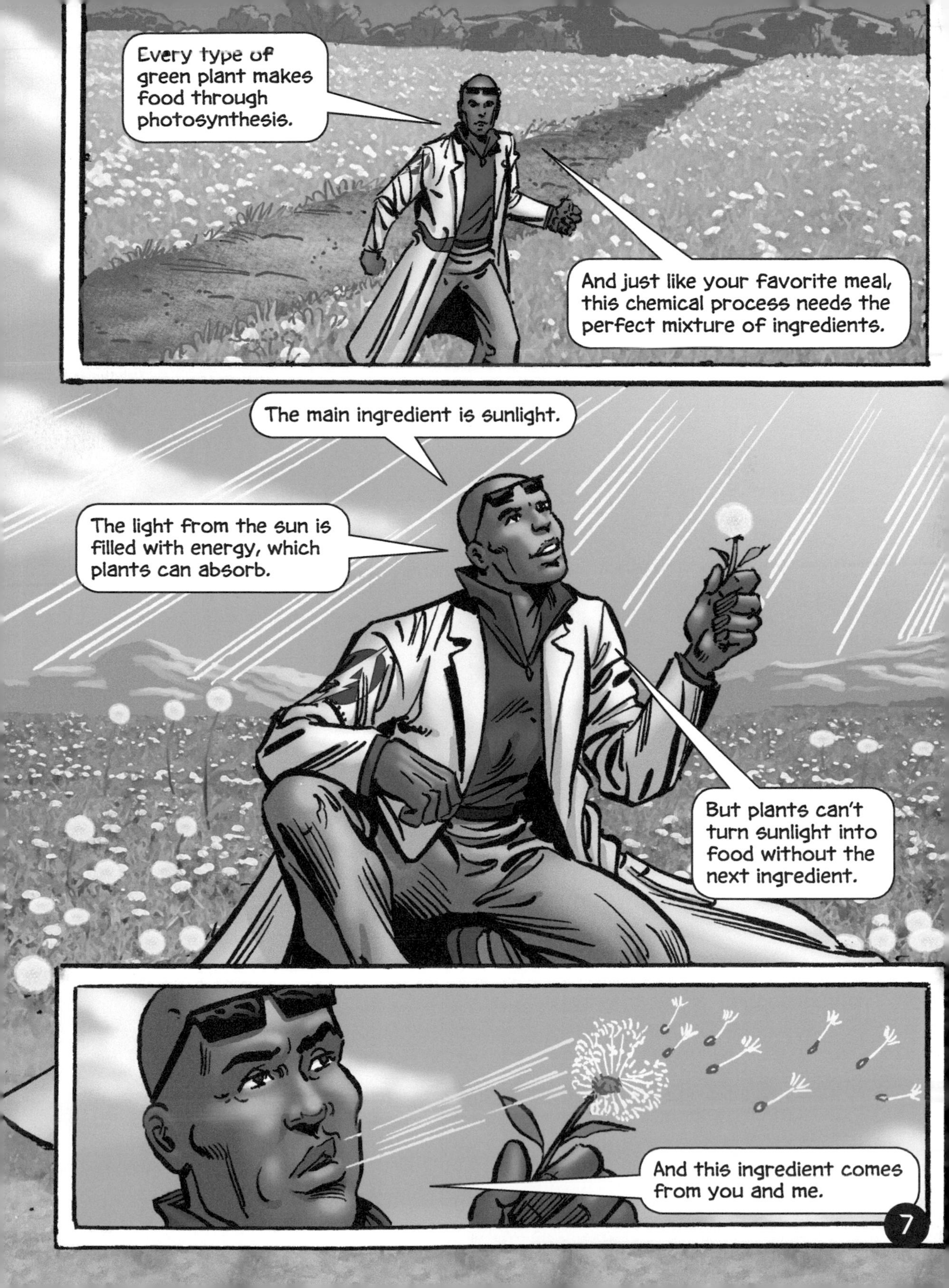
Every type of green plant makes food through photosynthesis.
And just like your favorite meal, this chemical process needs the perfect mixture of ingredients.
The main ingredient is sunlight.
The light from the sun is filled with energy, which plants can absorb.
But plants can't turn sunlight into food without the next ingredient.
And this ingredient comes from you and me.

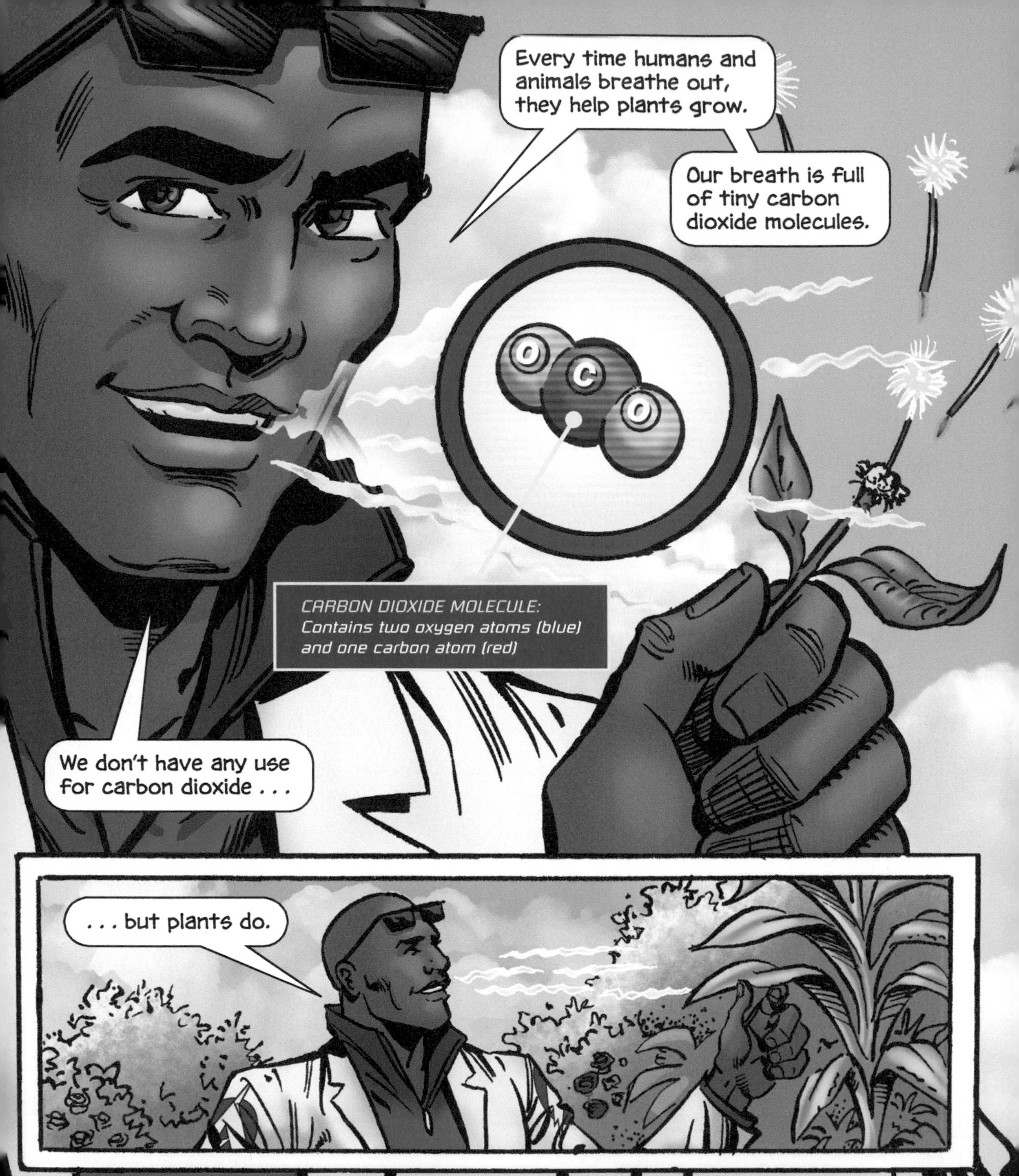
Every time humans and animals breathe out, they help plants grow.
Our breath is full of tiny carbon dioxide molecules.
O
C
O
CARBON DIOXIDE MOLECULE: Contains two oxygen atoms (blue) and one carbon atom (red)
We don't have any use for carbon dioxide . . .
. . . but plants do.

DEFINITION

carbon dioxide (KAHR-buhn dye-AHK-side)
A colorless, odorless gas that people and animals breathe out.

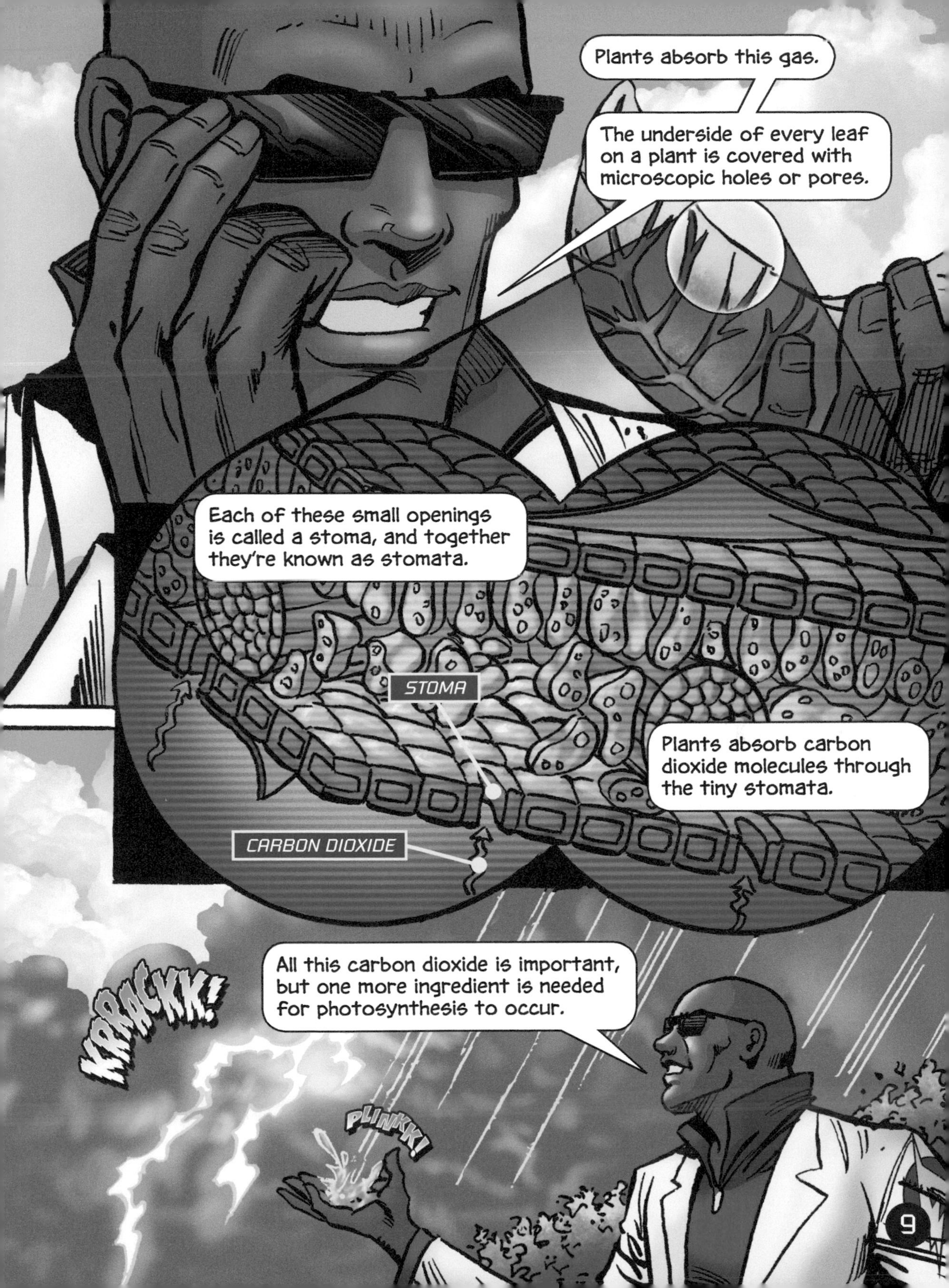
Plants absorb this gas.
The underside of every leaf on a plant is covered with microscopic holes or pores.
Each of these small openings is called a stoma, and together they're known as stomata.
STOMA
CARBON DIOXIDE
Plants absorb carbon dioxide molecules through the tiny stomata.
KRRACKK!
All this carbon dioxide is important, but one more ingredient is needed for photosynthesis to occur.
PLINKK!

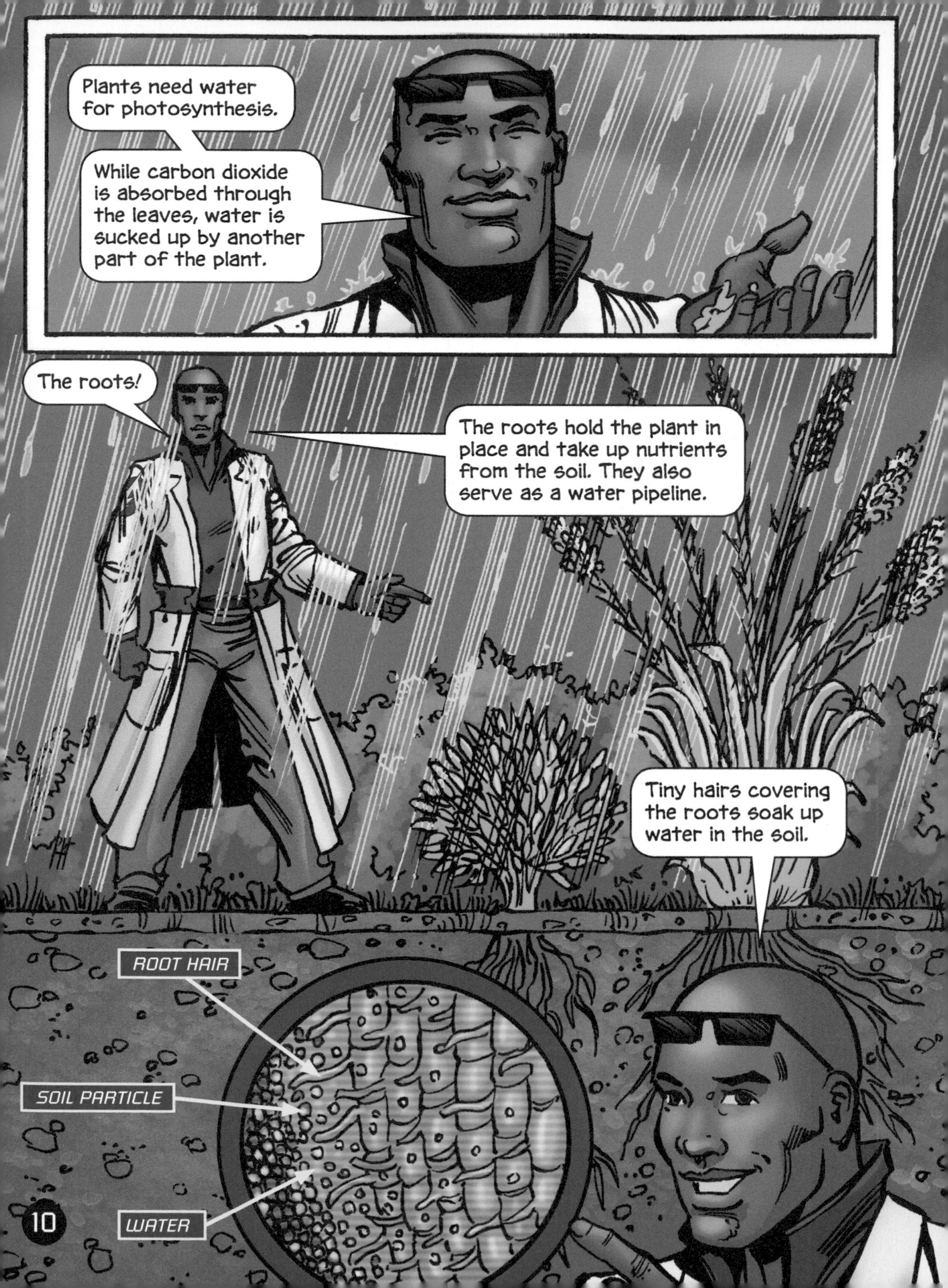
Plants need water for photosynthesis.
While carbon dioxide is absorbed through the leaves, water is sucked up by another part of the plant.
The roots!
The roots hold the plant in place and take up nutrients from the soil. They also serve as a water pipeline.
Tiny hairs covering the roots soak up water in the soil.
ROOT HAIR
SOIL PARTICLE
WATER

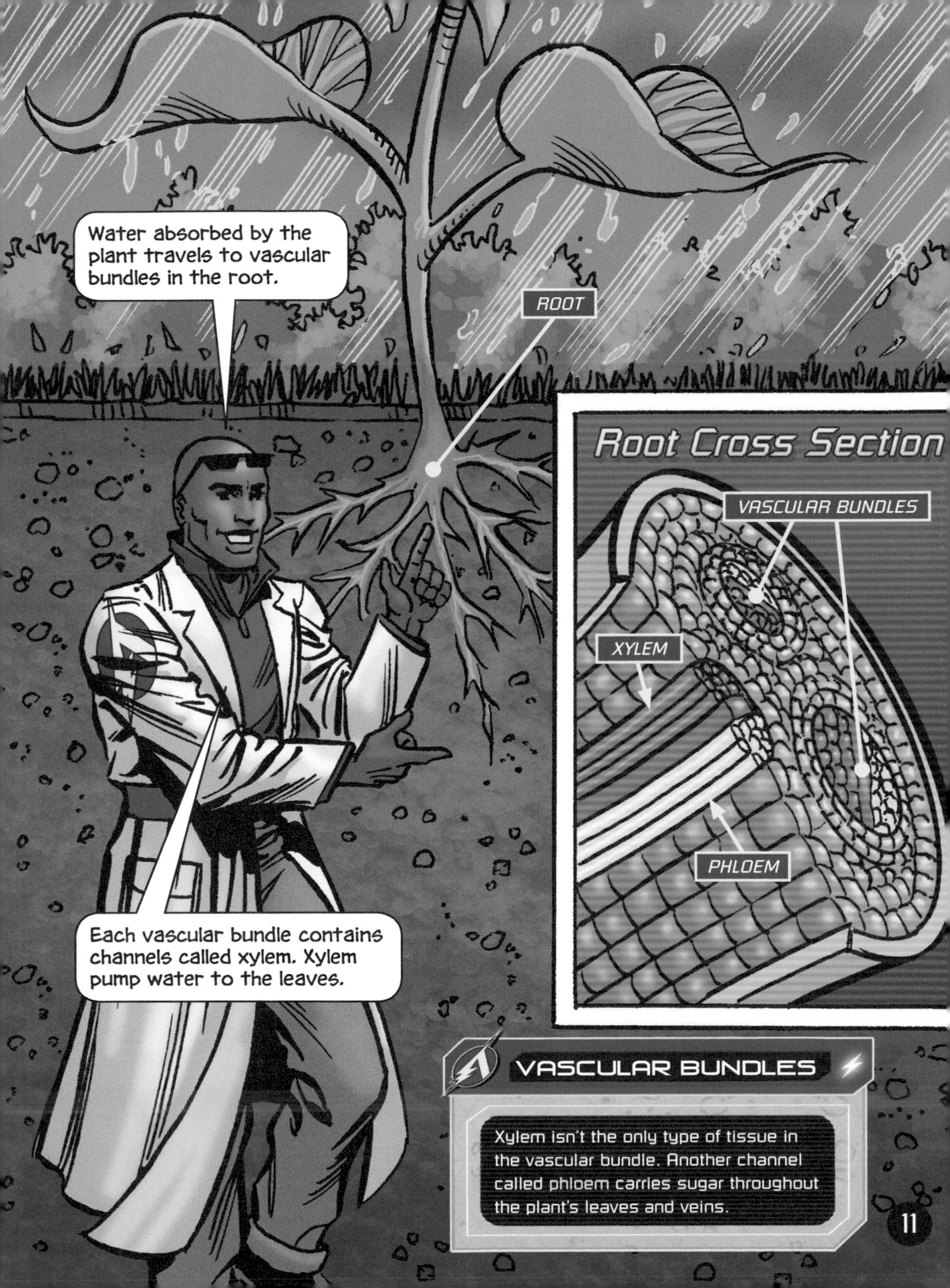
Water absorbed by the plant travels to vascular bundles in the root.
ROOT
Root Cross Section
VASCULAR BUNDLES
XYLEM
PHLOEM
Each vascular bundle contains channels called xylem. Xylem pump water to the leaves.
VASCULAR BUNDLES
Xylem isn't the only type of tissue in the vascular bundle. Another channel called phloem carries sugar throughout the plant's leaves and veins.

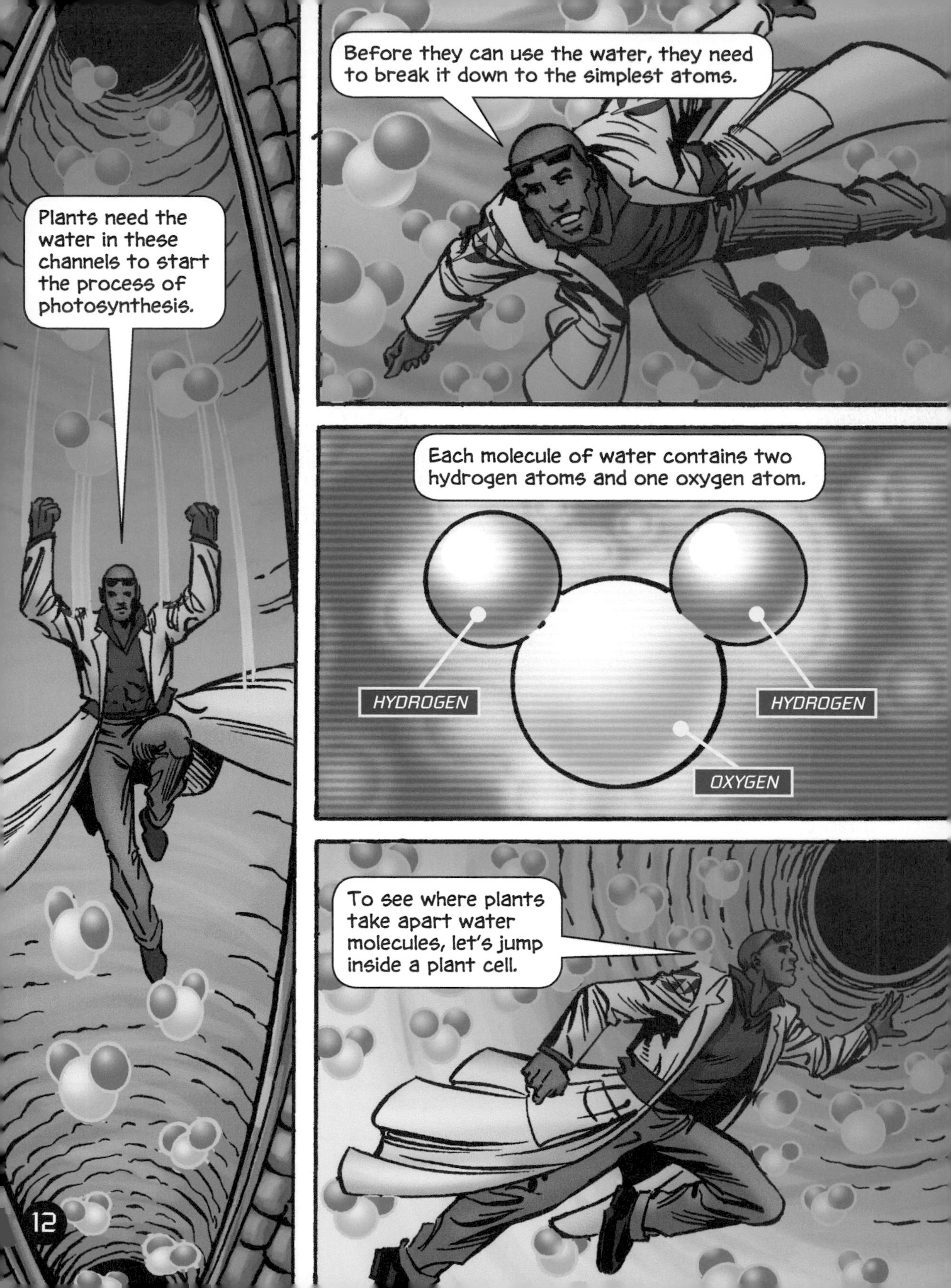

Plants need the water in these channels to start the process of photosynthesis.
Before they can use the water, they need to break it down to the simplest atoms.
Each molecule of water contains two hydrogen atoms and one oxygen atom.
HYDROGEN
HYDROGEN
OXYGEN
To see where plants take apart water molecules, let's jump inside a plant cell.

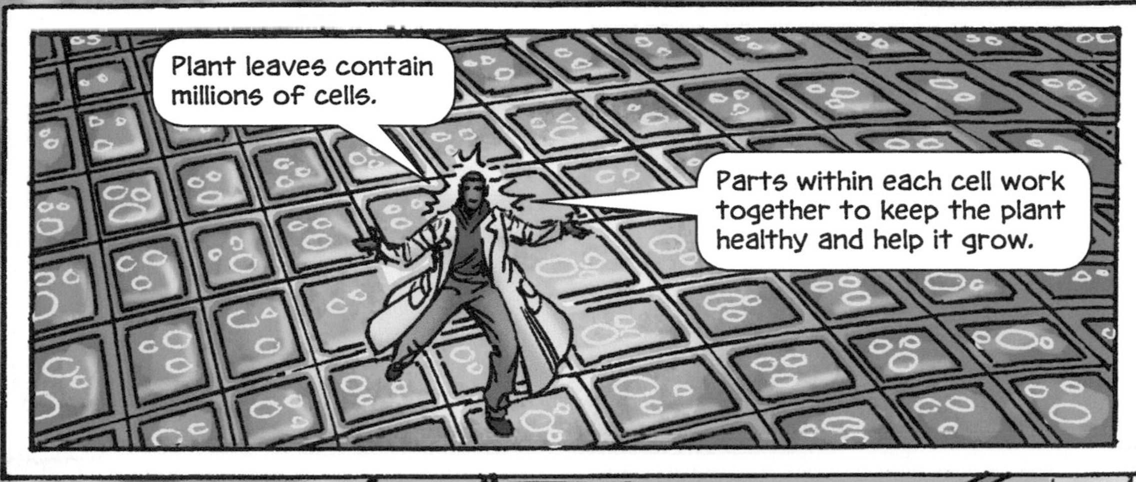
Plant leaves contain millions of cells.
Parts within each cell work together to keep the plant healthy and help it grow.

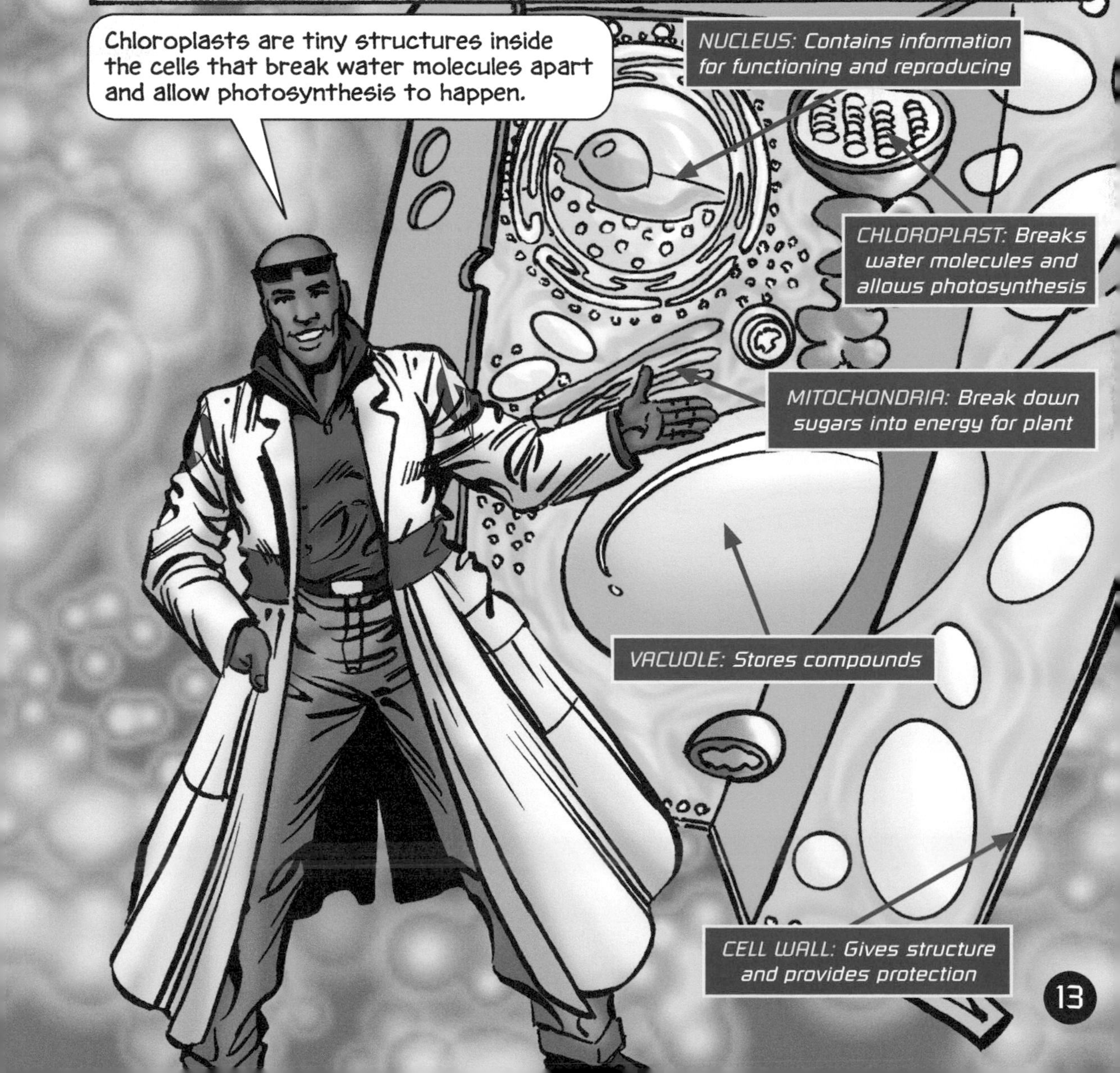
Chloroplasts are tiny structures inside the cells that break water molecules apart and allow photosynthesis to happen.
NUCLEUS: Contains information for functioning and reproducing
CHLOROPLAST: Breaks water molecules and allows photosynthesis
MITOCHONDRIA: Break down sugars into energy for plant
VACUOLE: Stores compounds
CELL WALL: Gives structure and provides protection

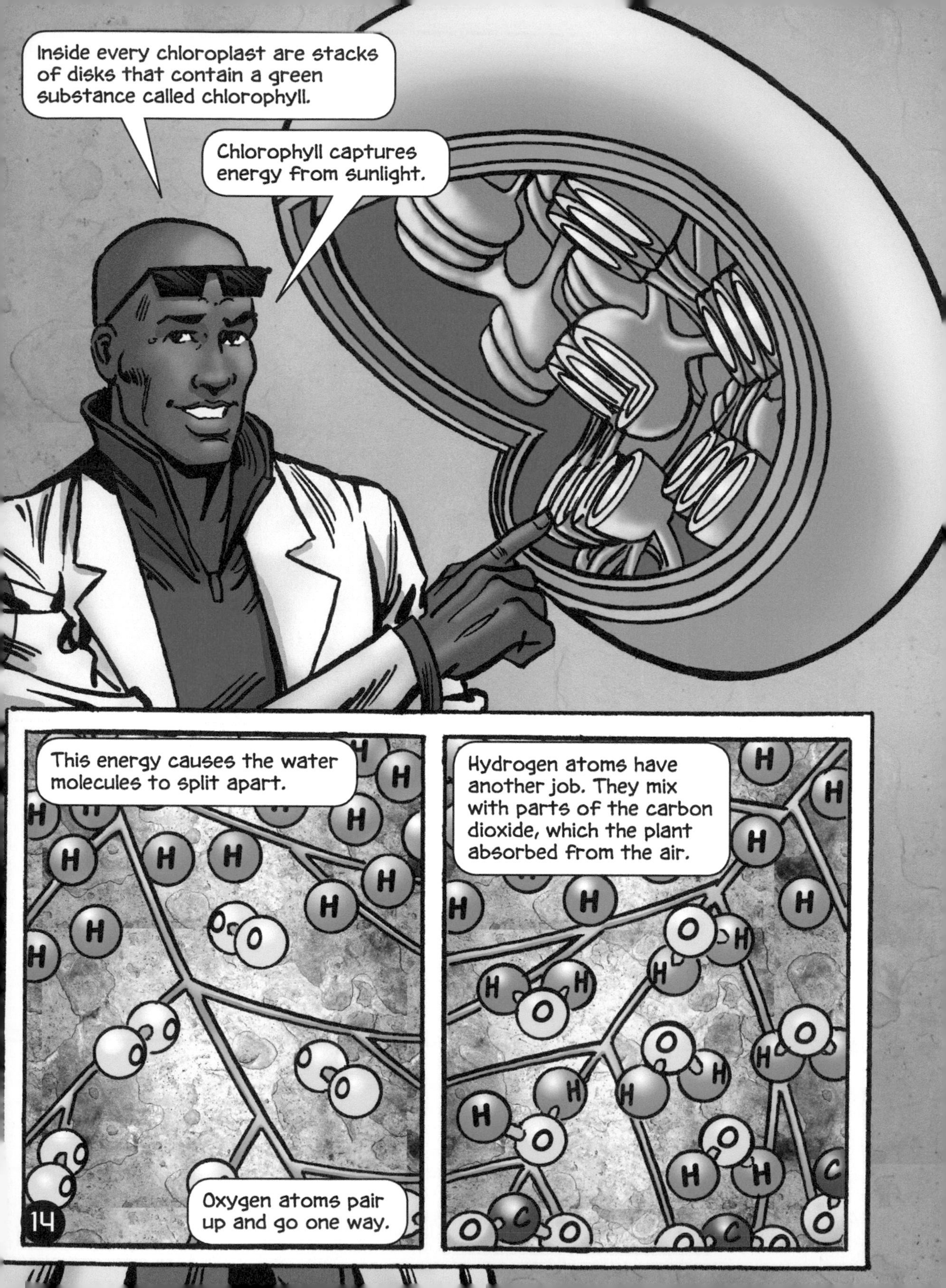
Inside every chloroplast are stacks of disks that contain a green substance called chlorophyll.
Chlorophyll captures energy from sunlight.
This energy causes the water molecules to split apart.
Oxygen atoms pair up and go one way.
Hydrogen atoms have another job. They mix with parts of the carbon dioxide, which the plant absorbed from the air.

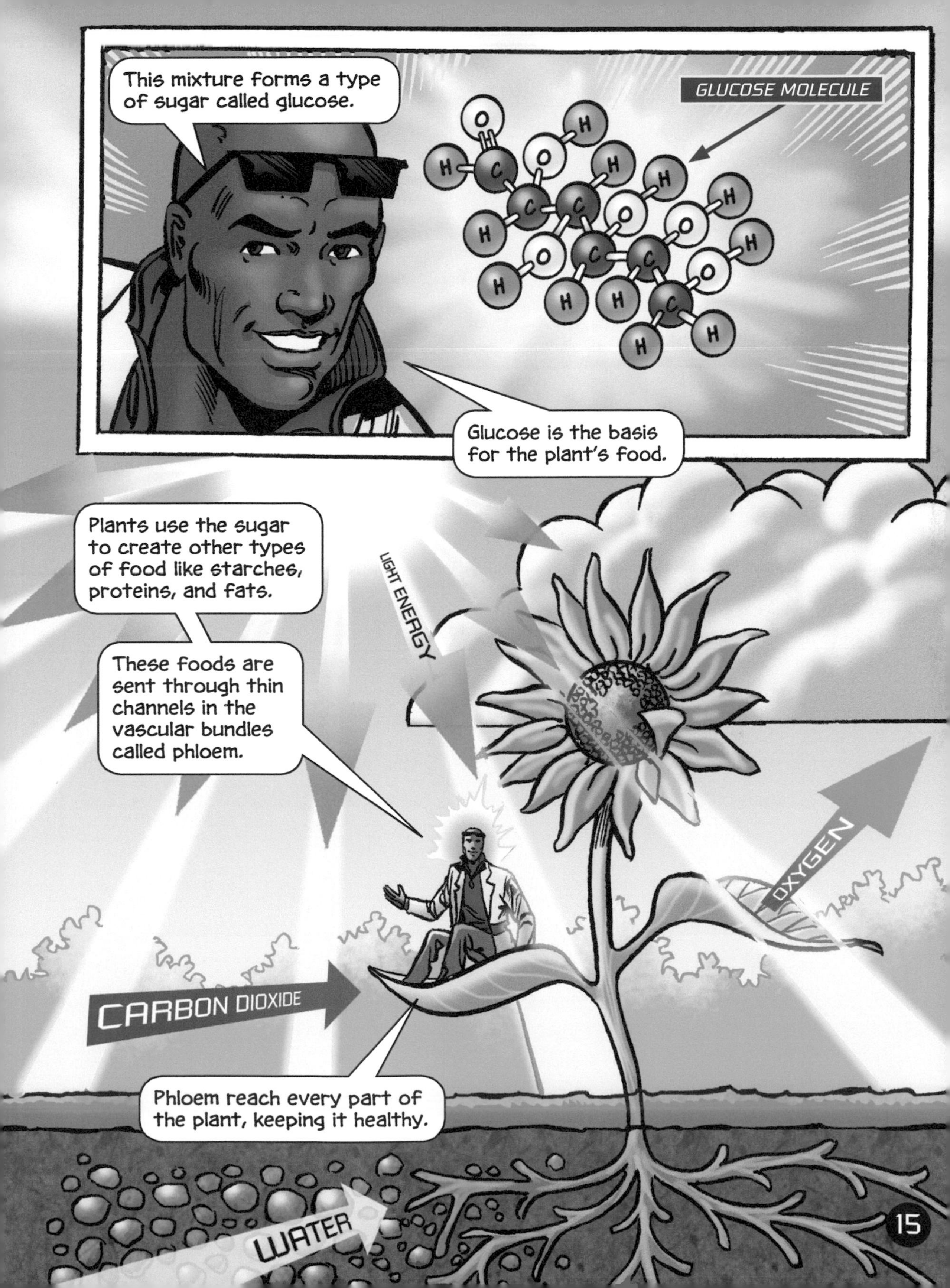
This mixture forms a type of sugar called glucose.
GLUCOSE MOLECULE
Glucose is the basis for the plant's food.
Plants use the sugar to create other types of food like starches, proteins, and fats.
LIGHT ENERGY
These foods are sent through thin channels in the vascular bundles called phloem.
OXYGEN
CARBON DIOXIDE
Phloem reach every part of the plant, keeping it healthy.
WATER

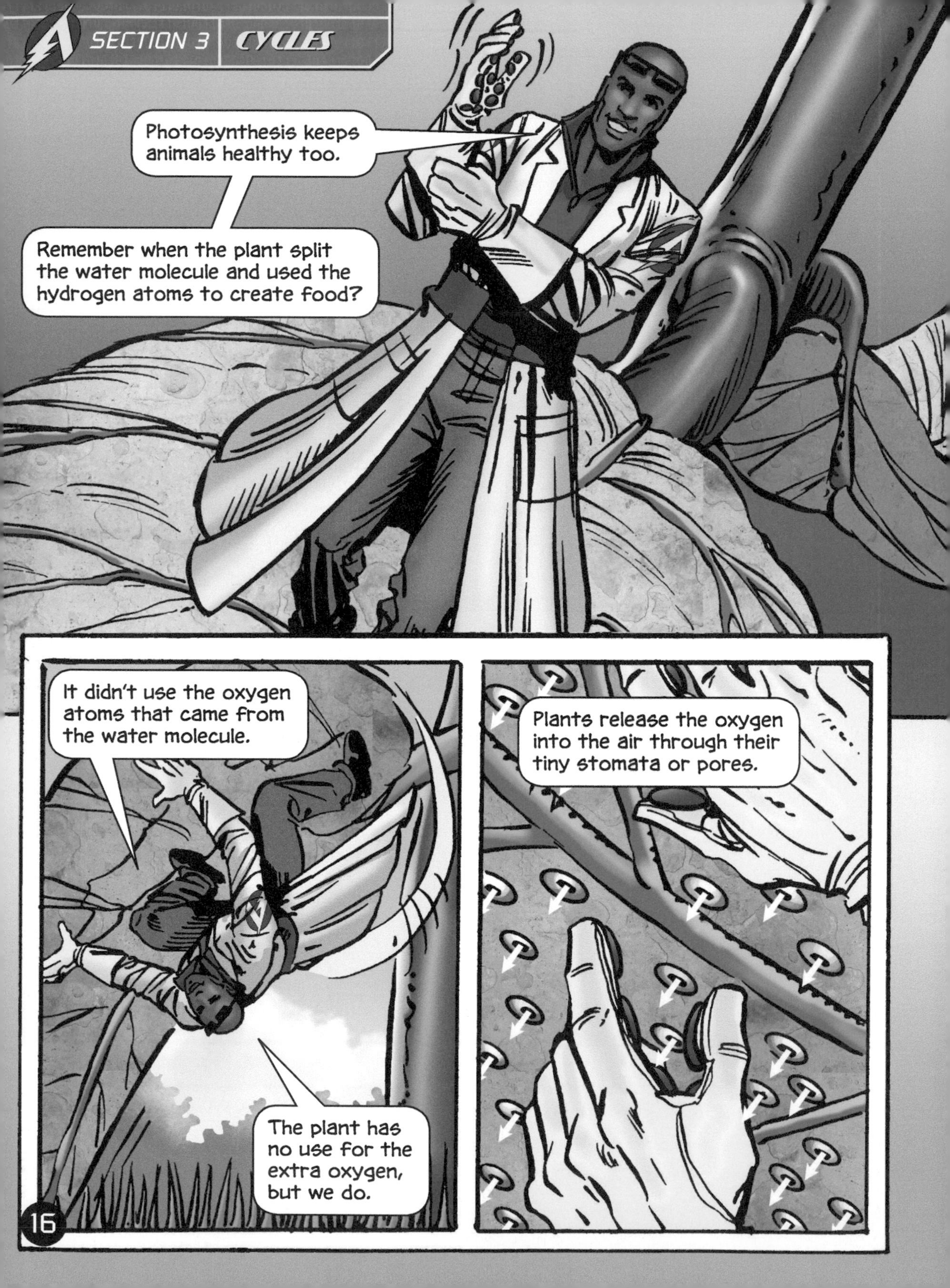
Photosynthesis keeps animals healthy too.
Remember when the plant split the water molecule and used the hydrogen atoms to create food?
It didn't use the oxygen atoms that came from the water molecule.
The plant has no use for the extra oxygen, but we do.
Plants release the oxygen into the air through their tiny stomata or pores.

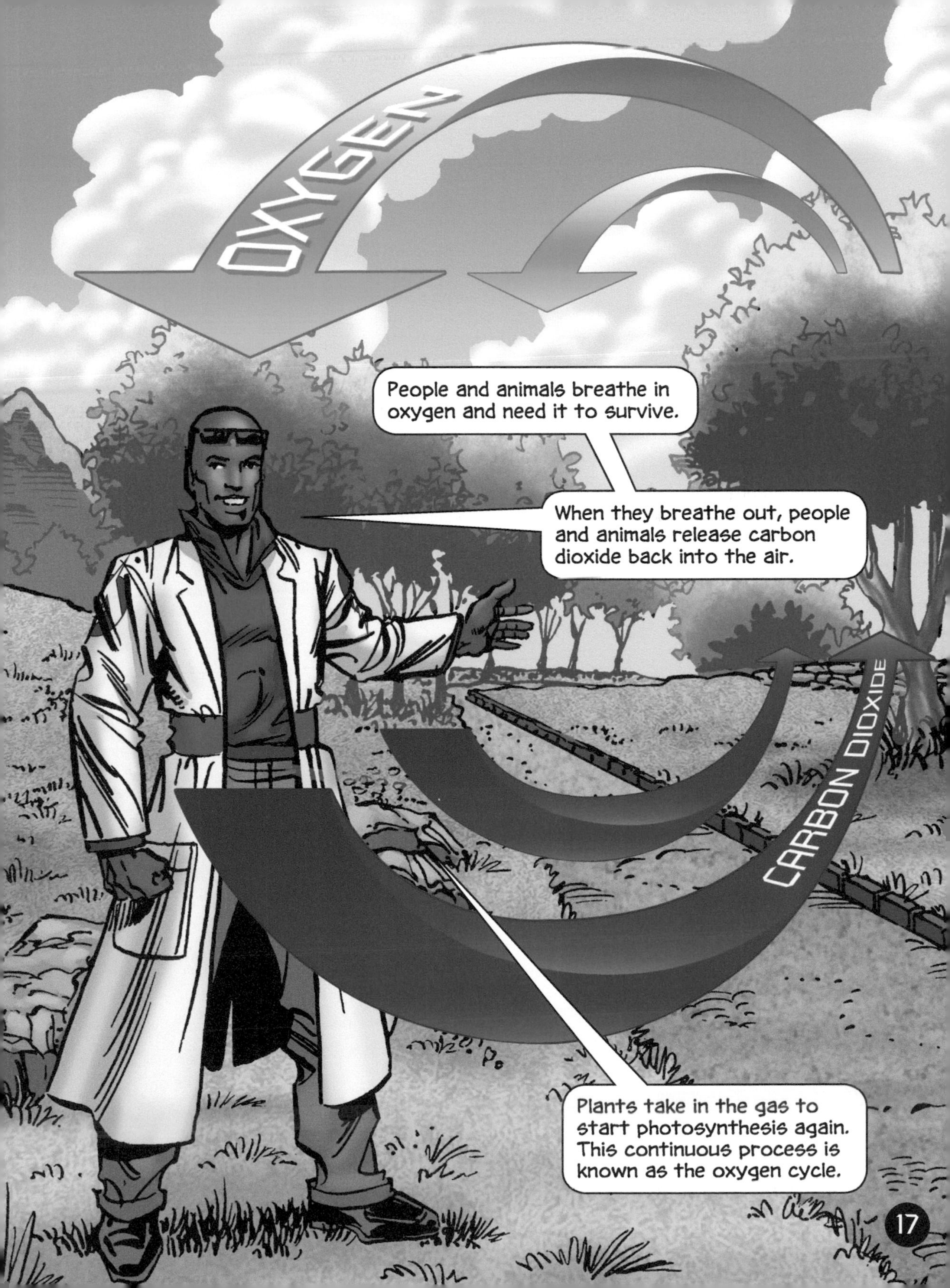

OXYGEN
People and animals breathe in oxygen and need it to survive.
When they breathe out, people and animals release carbon dioxide back into the air.
CARBON DIOXIDE
Plants take in the gas to start photosynthesis again. This continuous process is known as the oxygen cycle.

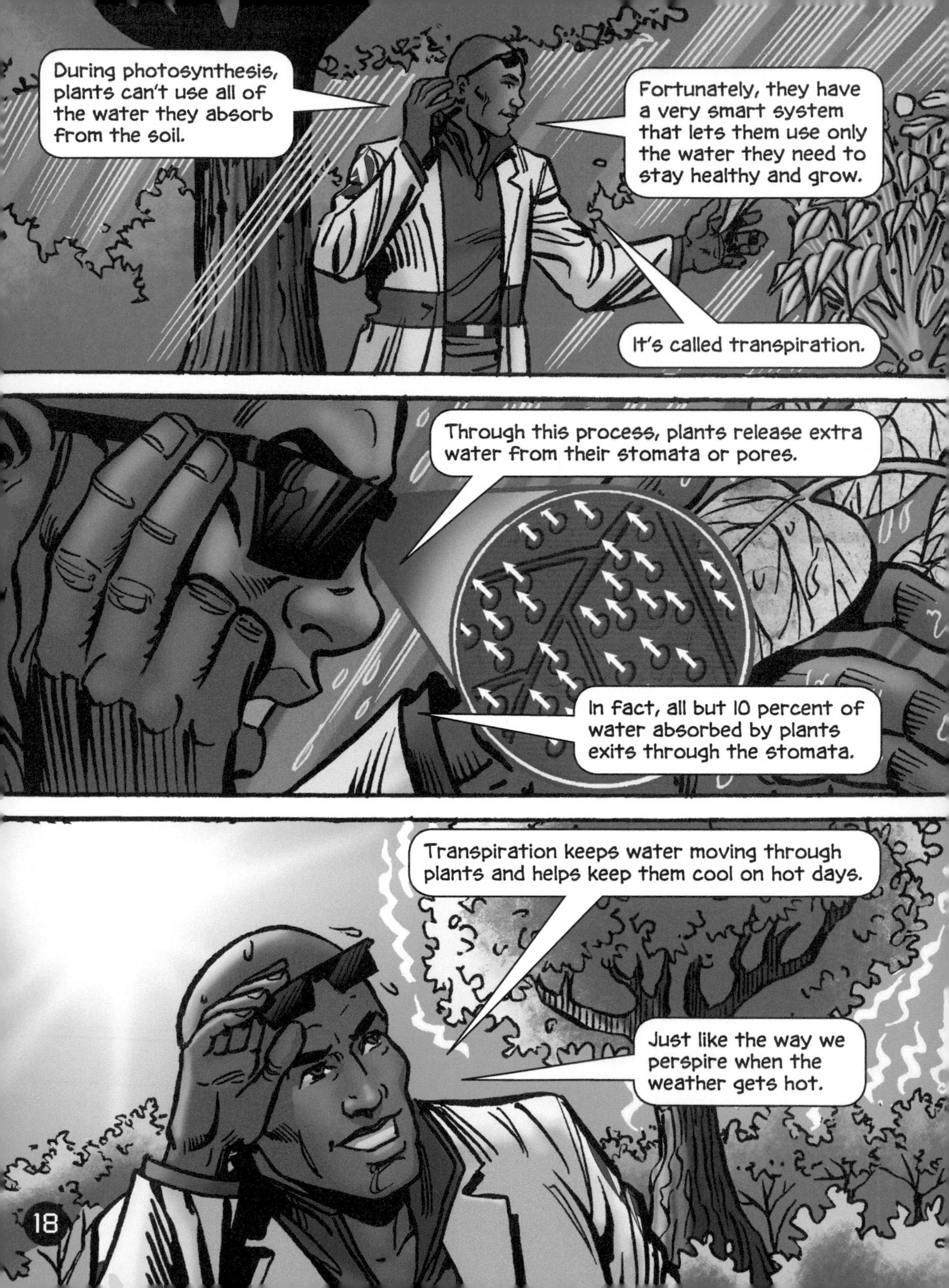
During photosynthesis, plants can't use all of the water they absorb from the soil.
Fortunately, they have a very smart system that lets them use only the water they need to stay healthy and grow.
It's called transpiration.
Through this process, plants release extra water from their stomata or pores.
In fact, all but 10 percent of water absorbed by plants exits through the stomata.
Transpiration keeps water moving through plants and helps keep them cool on hot days.
Just like the way we perspire when the weather gets hot.

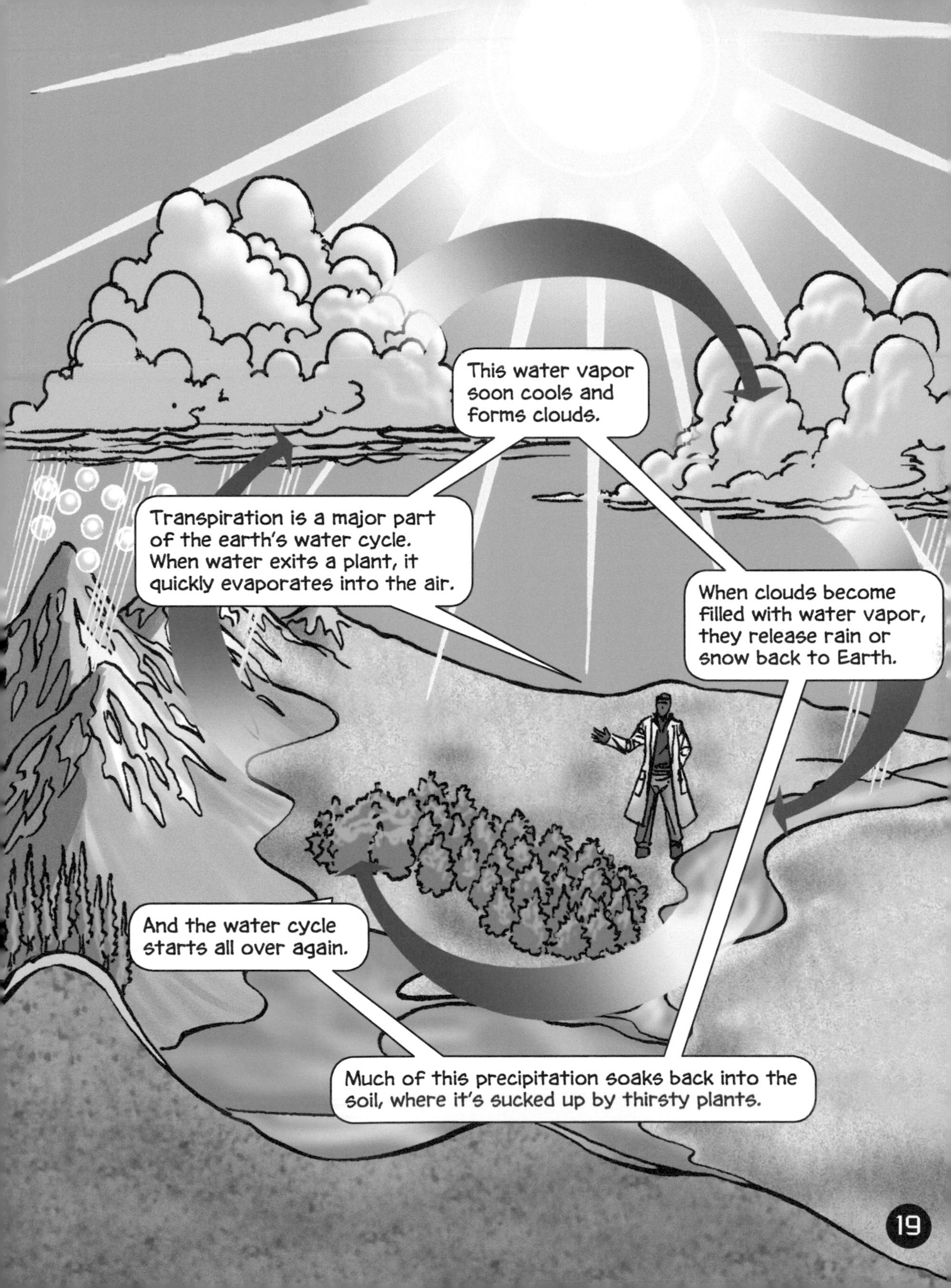
This water vapor soon cools and forms clouds.
Transpiration is a major part of the earth's water cycle. When water exits a plant, it quickly evaporates into the air.
When clouds become filled with water vapor, they release rain or snow back to Earth.
And the water cycle starts all over again.
Much of this precipitation soaks back into the soil, where it's sucked up by thirsty plants.

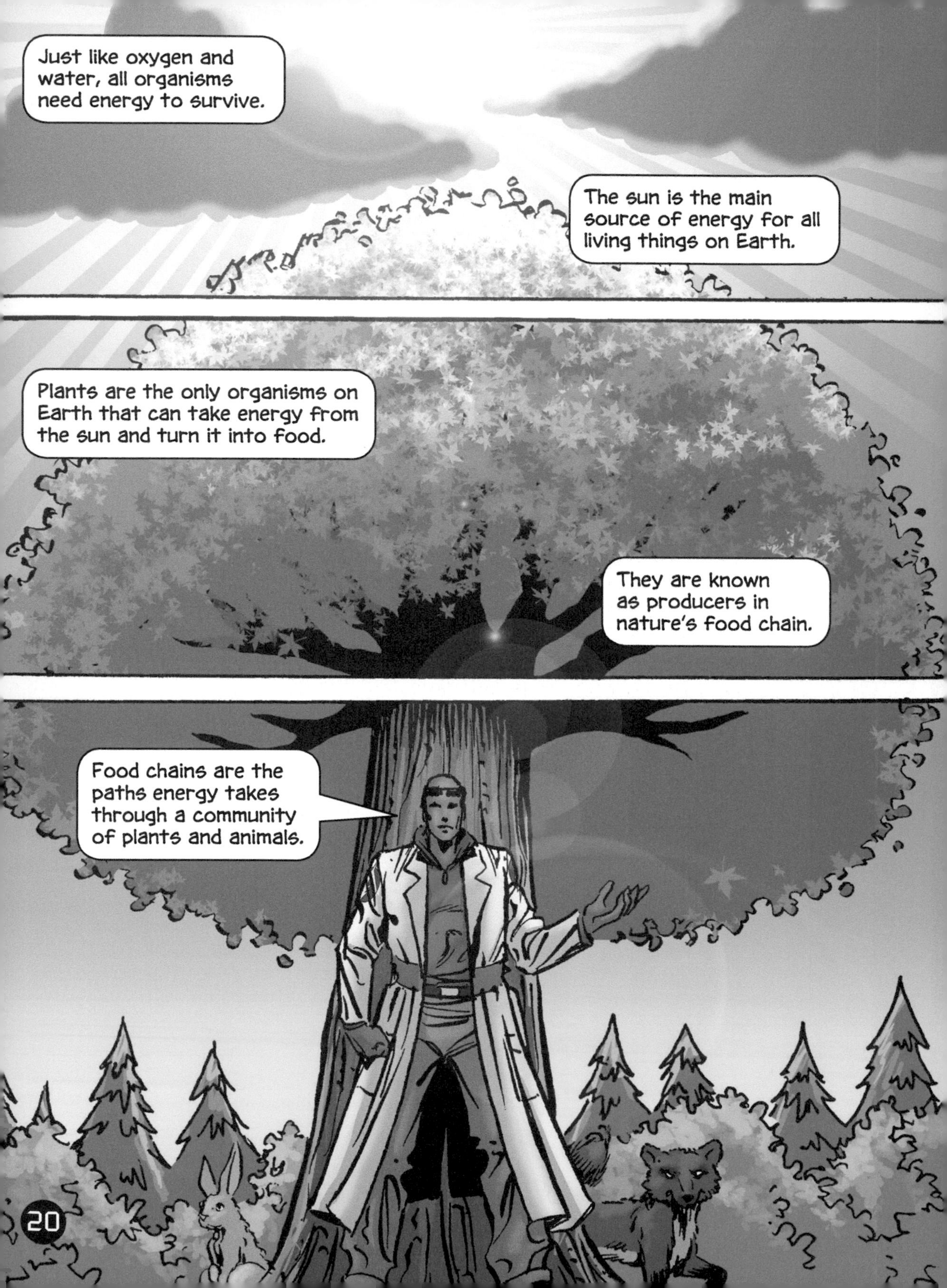
Just like oxygen and water, all organisms need energy to survive.
The sun is the main source of energy for all living things on Earth.
Plants are the only organisms on Earth that can take energy from the sun and turn it into food.
They are known as producers in nature's food chain.
Food chains are the paths energy takes through a community of plants and animals.

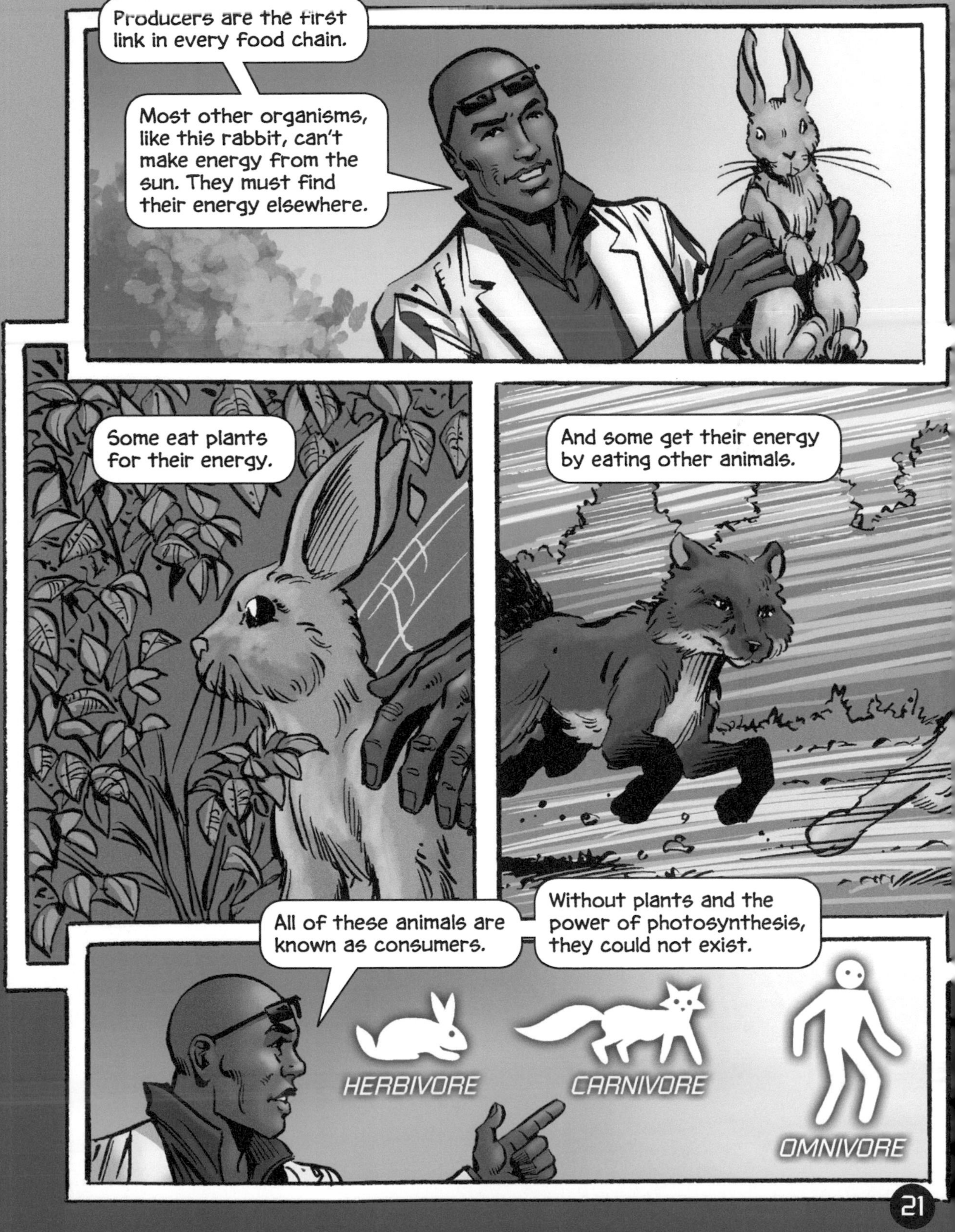
Producers are the first link in every food chain.
Most other organisms, like this rabbit, can't make energy from the sun. They must find their energy elsewhere.
Some eat plants for their energy.
And some get their energy by eating other animals.
All of these animals are known as consumers.
Without plants and the power of photosynthesis, they could not exist.
HERBIVORE
CARNIVORE
OMNIVORE

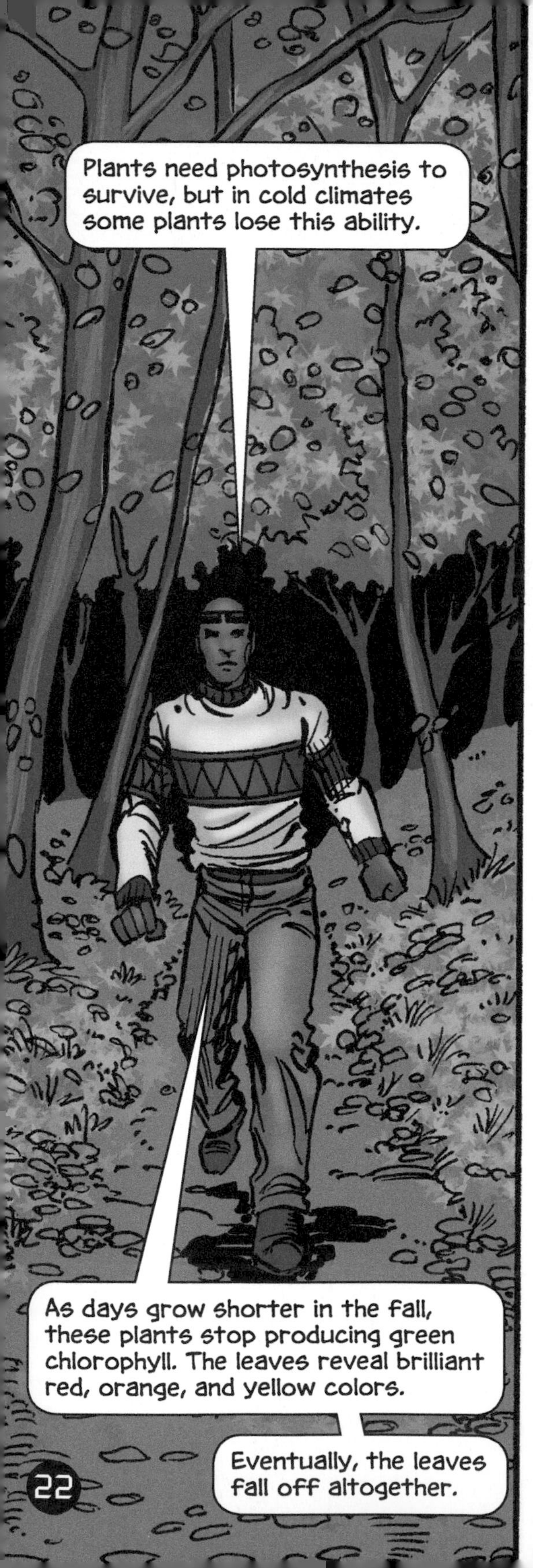
Plants need photosynthesis to survive, but in cold climates some plants lose this ability.
As days grow shorter in the fall, these plants stop producing green chlorophyll. The leaves reveal brilliant red, orange, and yellow colors.
Eventually, the leaves fall off altogether.

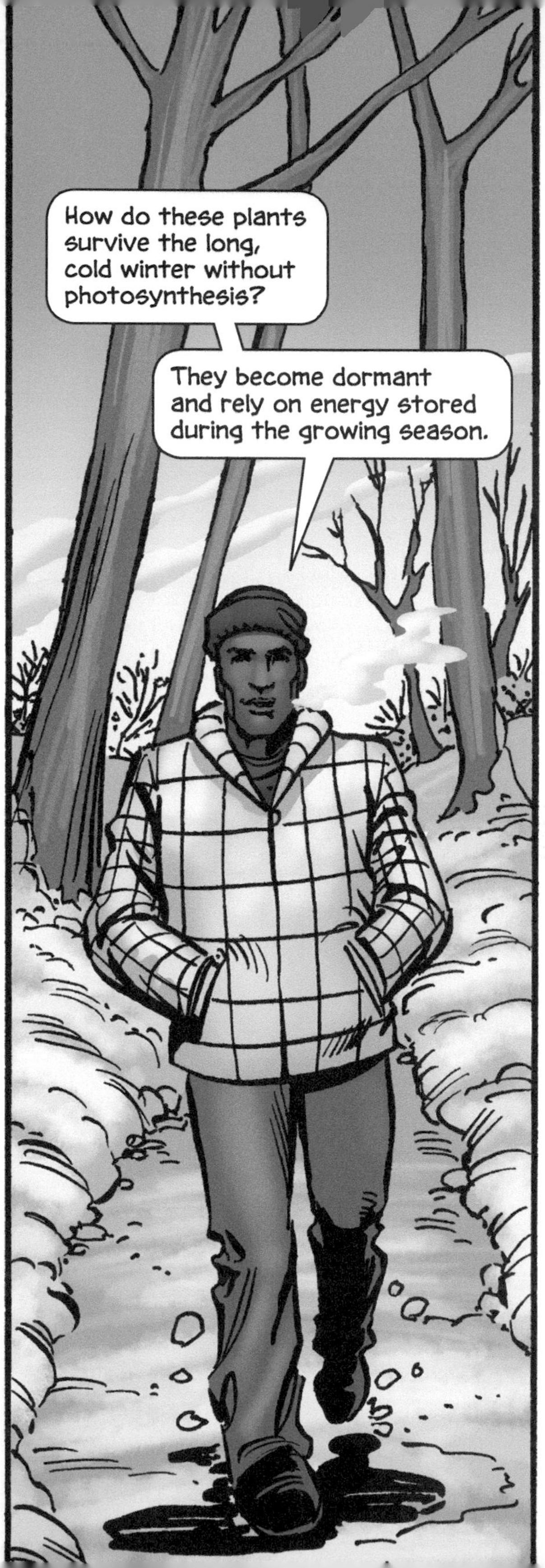
How do these plants survive the long, cold winter without photosynthesis?
They become dormant and rely on energy stored during the growing season.

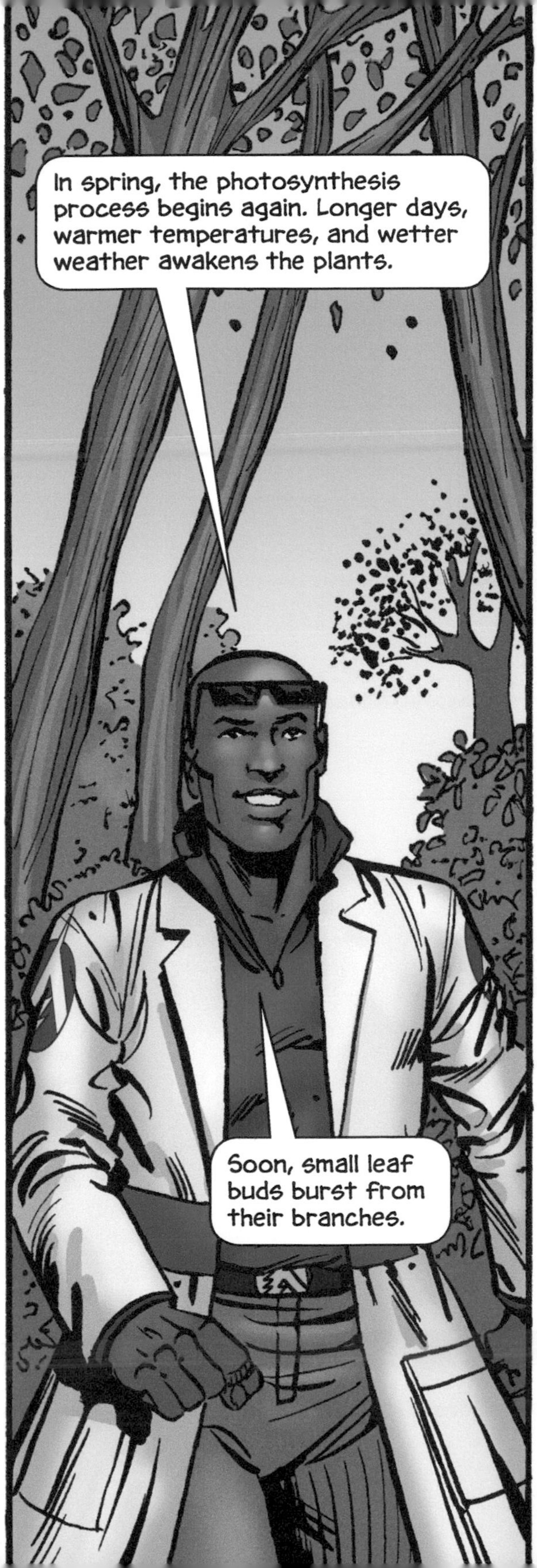
In spring, the photosynthesis process begins again. Longer days, warmer temperatures, and wetter weather awakens the plants.
Soon, small leaf buds burst from their branches.
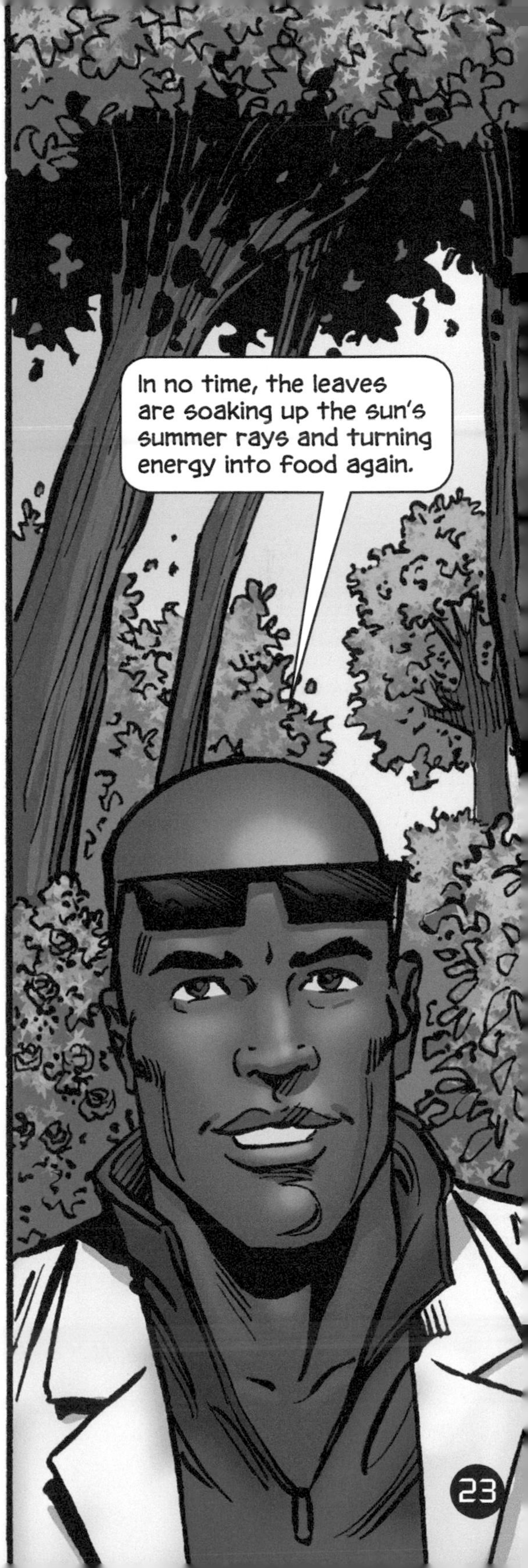
In no time, the leaves are soaking up the sun's summer rays and turning energy into food again.

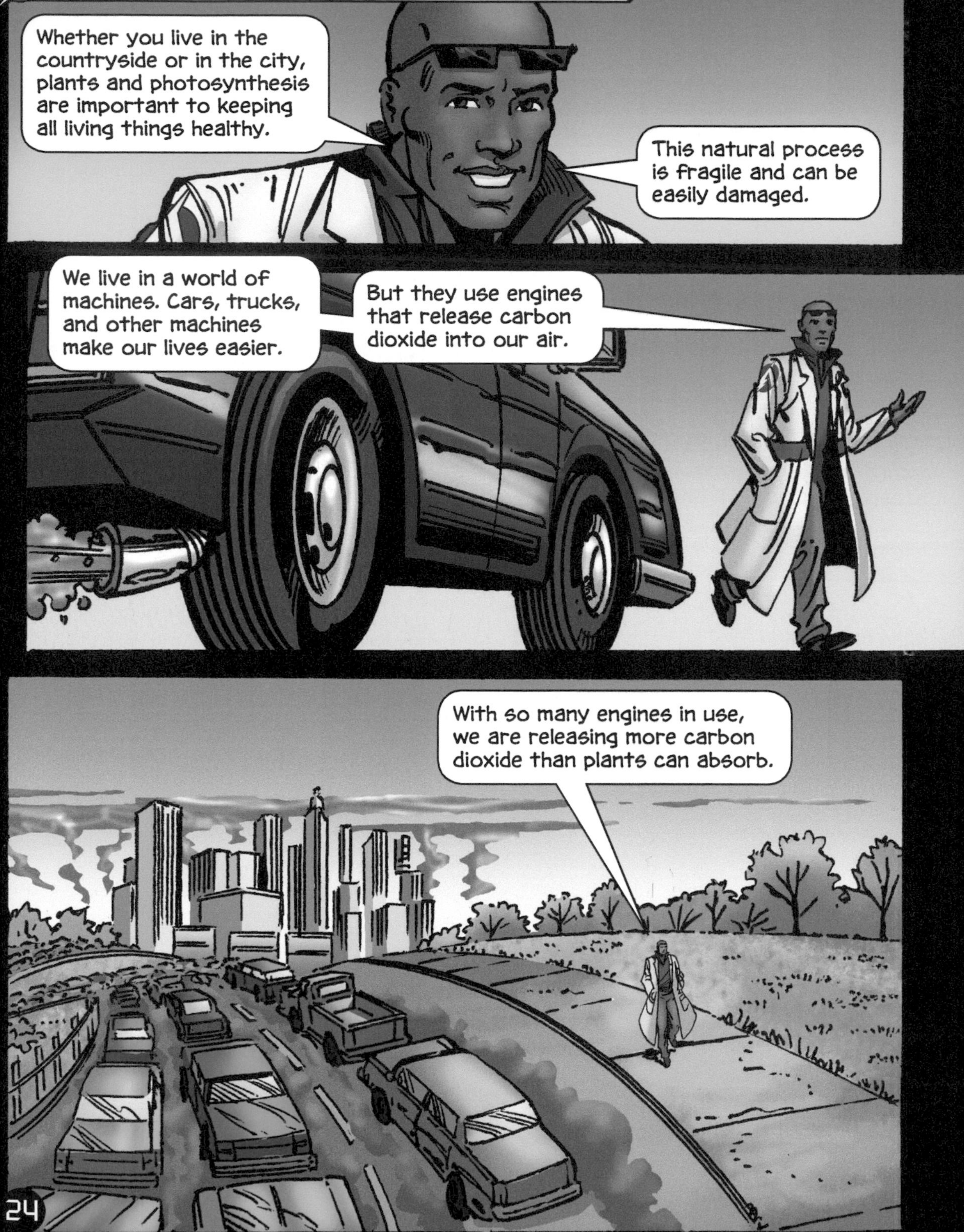
Whether you live in the countryside or in the city, plants and photosynthesis are important to keeping all living things healthy.
This natural process is fragile and can be easily damaged.
We live in a world of machines. Cars, trucks, and other machines make our lives easier.
But they use engines that release carbon dioxide into our air.
With so many engines in use, we are releasing more carbon dioxide than plants can absorb.

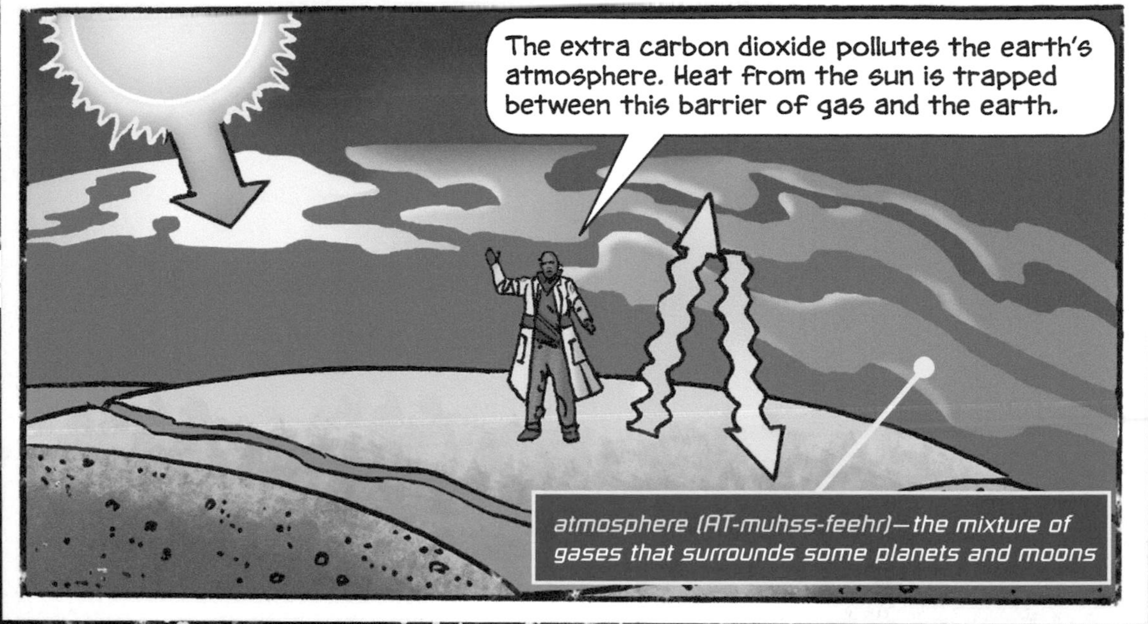
The extra carbon dioxide pollutes the earth's atmosphere. Heat from the sun is trapped between this barrier of gas and the earth.
atmosphere (AT-muhss-feehr)—the mixture of gases that surrounds some planets and moons

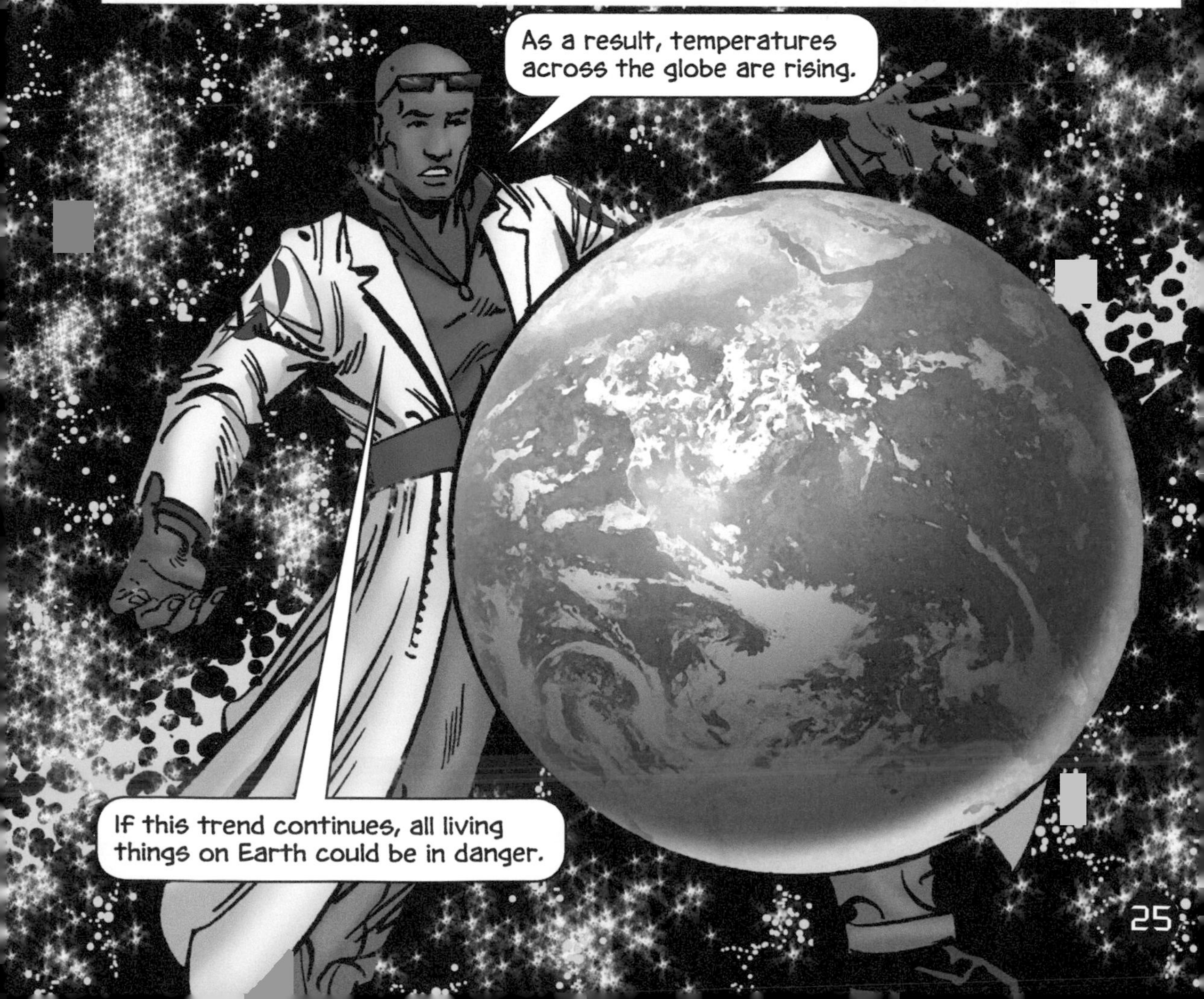
As a result, temperatures across the globe are rising.
If this trend continues, all living things on Earth could be in danger.

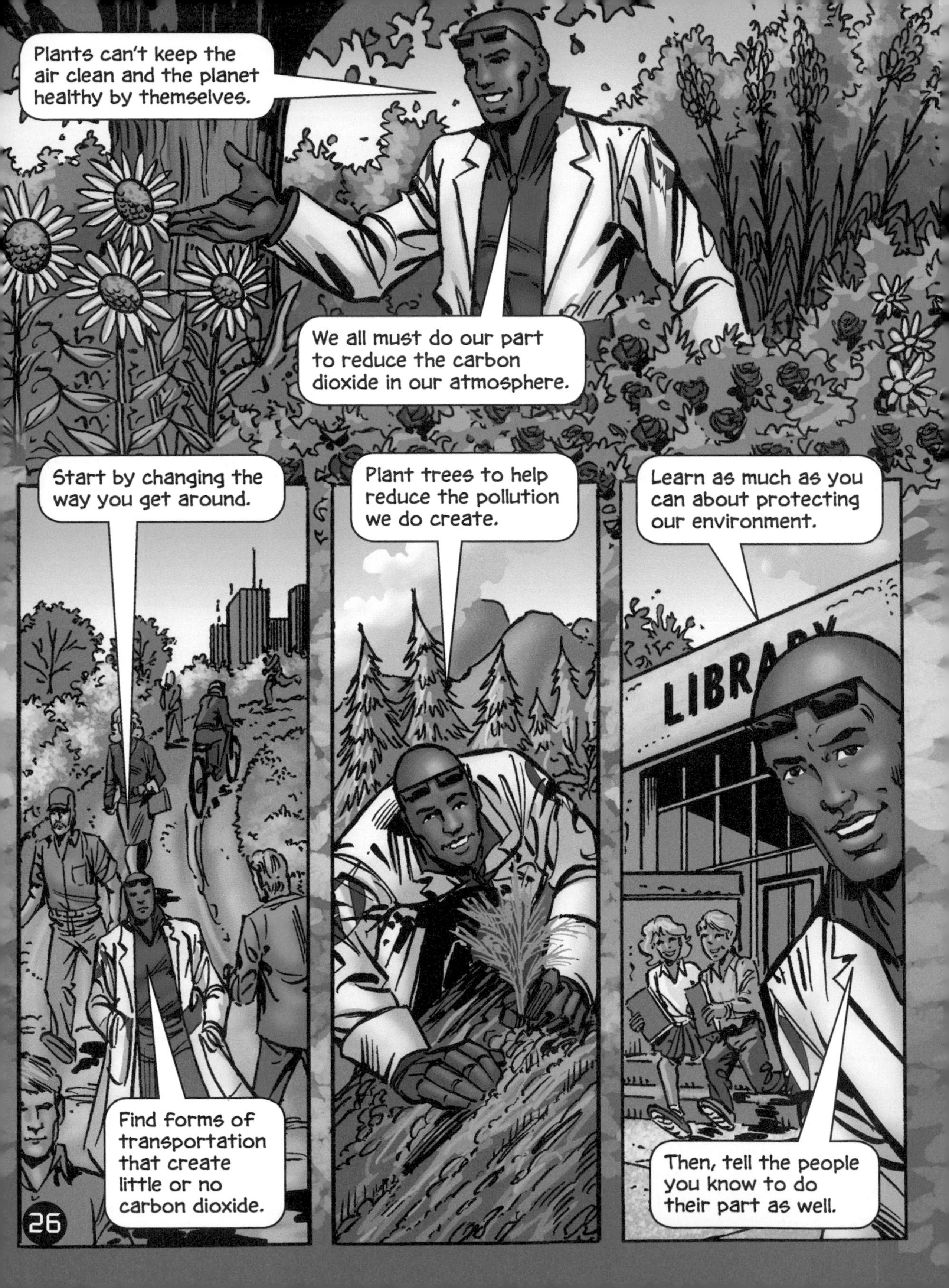
Plants can't keep the air clean and the planet healthy by themselves.
We all must do our part to reduce the carbon dioxide in our atmosphere.
Start by changing the way you get around.
Find forms of transportation that create little or no carbon dioxide.
Plant trees to help reduce the pollution we do create.
Learn as much as you can about protecting our environment.
LIBRARY
Then, tell the people you know to do their part as well.

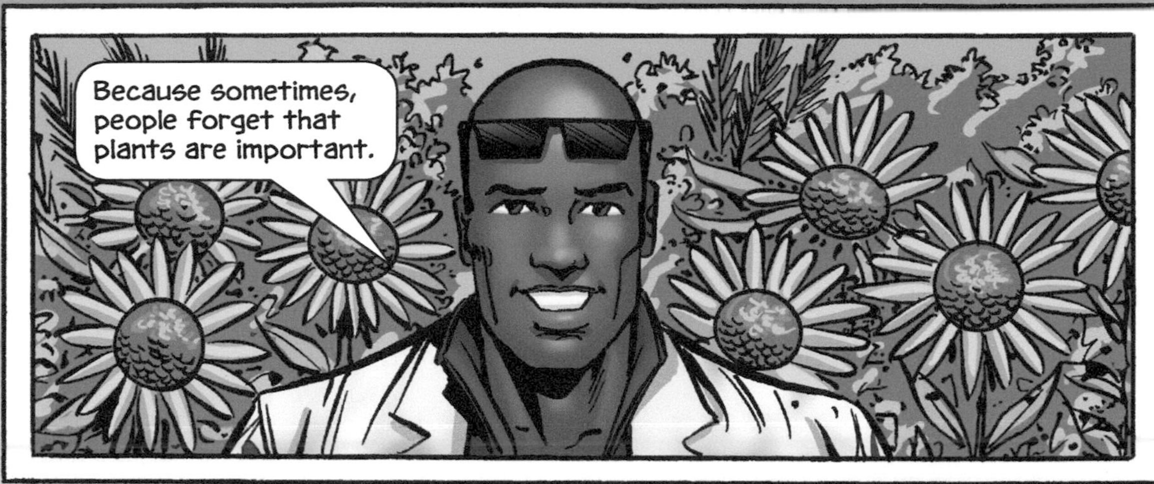
Because sometimes, people forget that plants are important.

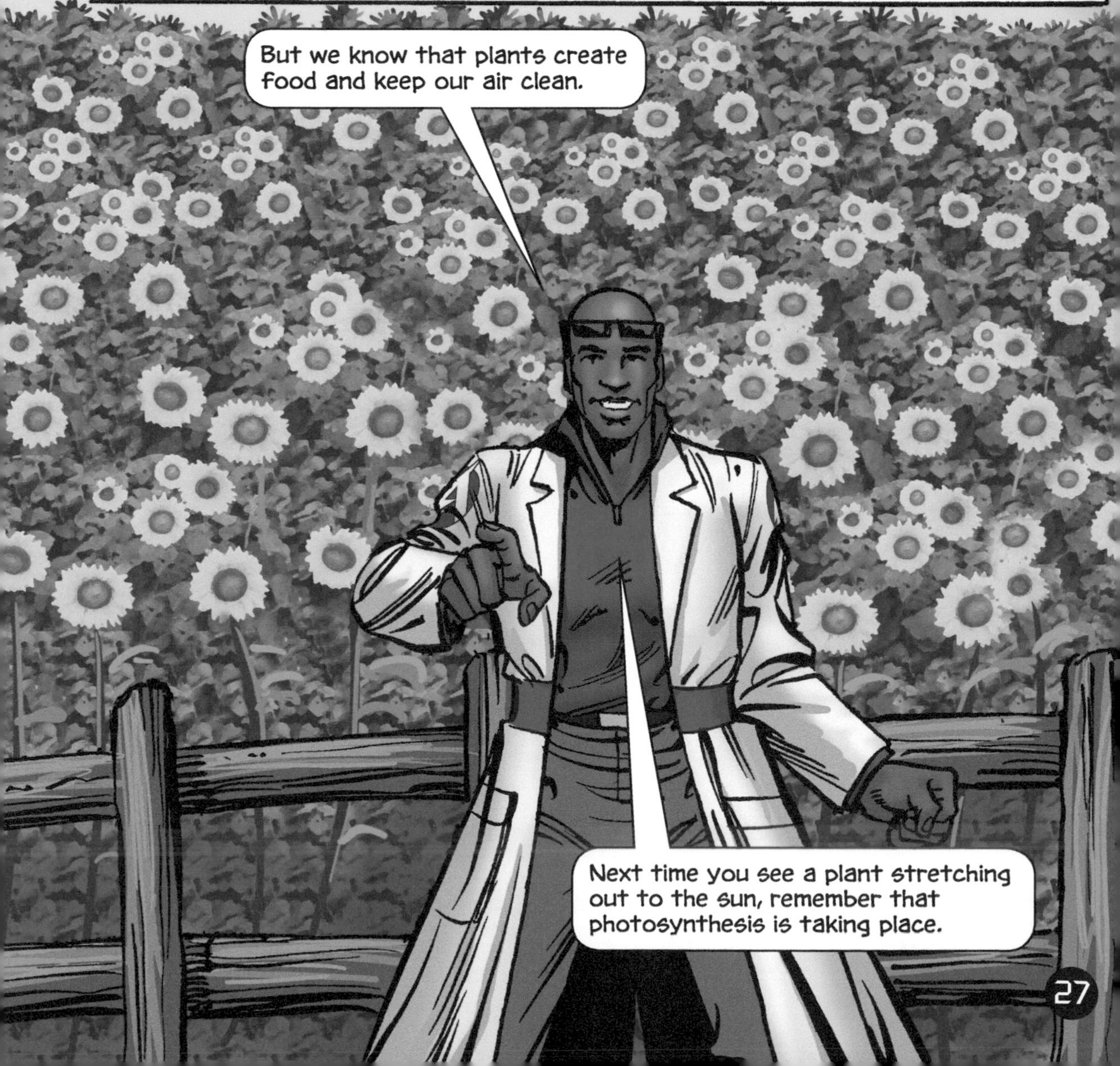
But we know that plants create food and keep our air clean.
Next time you see a plant stretching out to the sun, remember that photosynthesis is taking place.

MORE ABOUT
PHOTOSYNTHESIS

 The main source of energy for every living thing is more than 93 million miles (150 million kilometers) away. Fortunately, energy from the sun travels extremely fast and takes only eight minutes to reach our planet.

 Parts of the photosynthesis process can continue even without light from the sun. When the sun sets, plants still turn energy into sugars for food. This part of the process is known as the dark reaction phase.

 Our planet has a wide variety of plant life. In fact, more than 260,000 species of plants grow on Earth.

 The Indian pipe plant has no chlorophyll. The flowering plant is completely white and has been called corpse plant or ghost flower. Lacking the ability to create food, the Indian pipe absorbs energy through its roots from fungi.

 While some plants don't need sunlight, others don't need soil. Epiphyte plants dig their roots into trees or rocks for support. Moss, orchids, and other epiphytes often live high up on trees for better sunlight. Because of their location, they are sometimes called "air plants."

 Planting a tree can have a major impact. One grown tree produces enough oxygen to support four people for a year.

 Plants are the earth's only producers. Most other organisms are divided into three types of consumers:

Herbivores—animals that eat only plants
Carnivores—animals that eat other animals
Omnivores—animals that eat both plants and animals

 Plants can be carnivores. Some plants, including Venus flytraps and monkey cups, live where few nutrients are in the soil. They capture insects in their traps for food.

PLANT POWER!

Grow your knowledge of plant power by studying the effects of light on leaves. How illuminating!

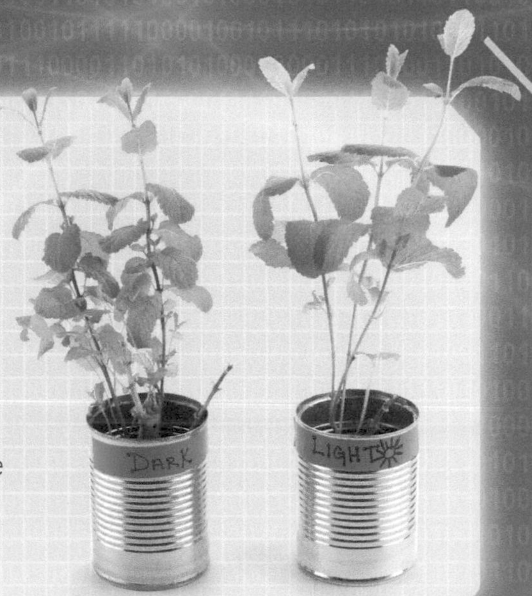
DARK
LIGHT

WHAT YOU NEED:

- 2 small plants, such as radish seedlings, basil, or mint
- paper and pencil
- 2 empty soup cans
- soil
- masking tape
- marker
- water

WHAT YOU DO:

1. Rinse the soil off the roots of one of your plants. Gently study the plant from the roots up to the leaves.
2. Try to identify each part of the plant and what it's used for. Draw a diagram of your plant on your paper.
3. Pot your plants into the cans, making sure the soil covers the roots completely.
4. Using the masking tape and marker, label one can "Light" and one "Dark."
5. Make a chart with two rows and 14 columns. Label one row "Light" and the other row "Dark." Number the columns 1 to 15 for each of the 14 days of your experiment.
6. Study your potted plants. Note what your plants look like in the Day 1 column.
7. Place the "Light" plant in a sunny window. Place the "Dark" plant in a dark closet.
8. For the next 14 days, water both plants a little bit every day, in equal amounts and at the same time of day. Record what each plant looks like on your chart for each day of the week. You may also want to sketch the plants' appearances along the way if you wish.
9. On day 14, compare the Light plant with the Dark plant. Using your knowledge of photosynthesis, what do you think has occurred? What connections can be made about chlorophyll and sunlight? Write them down.

DISCUSSION QUESTIONS

1. Max says the sunflowers are eating when the Sun shines on them. What does he mean by this? Explain your answer.

2. Plants provide for us in many ways. What are plants our source of? What would we be missing if plants weren't on Earth?

3. Why can some plants not make their own food during the winter? Discuss how they survive.

4. Plants can't use all of the carbon dioxide that people add to air. What can happen as a result of the extra carbon dioxide? What can people do to help?

WRITING PROMPTS

1. What is photosynthesis? Based on what you've read in the book, write a definition for photosynthesis in your own words.

2. Plants are a major part of two cycles. Make a chart with two columns—one for the oxygen cycle and one for the water cycle. List everything plants do in each cycle.

3. Create a recipe for photosynthesis as though it were from a science cookbook. What ingredients are needed for photosynthesis?

4. Photosynthesis results in products. Create a list of the products of photosynthesis. Pick one of the products and explain why it's important to you in one or two sentences.

TAKE A QUIZ!

GLOSSARY

atmosphere (AT-muhss-feehr)—the mixture of gases that surrounds Earth

atom (AT-uhm)—an element in its smallest form

carbon dioxide (KAHR-buhn dye-AHK-side)—a colorless, odorless gas that people and animals breathe out

chlorophyll (KLOER-uh-fil)—the green substance in plants that uses light to make food from carbon dioxide and water

hydrogen (HYE-druh-juhn)—a colorless gas that is lighter than air and burns easily

molecule (MOL-uh-kyool)—the atoms making up the smallest unit of a substance; H_2O is a molecule of water.

oxygen (OK-suh-juhn)—a colorless gas in the air that people and animals need to breathe

precipitation (pri-sip-i-TAY-shuhn)—water that falls from clouds to the earth's surface; precipitation can be rain, hail, sleet, or snow.

transpiration (transs-puh-RAY-shuhn)—the process by which plants give off moisture into the atmosphere

vascular (VASS-kew-luhr)—a system of channels for transporting fluids through plants

READ MORE

Higgins, Nadia. *Experiments with Photosynthesis*. Lightning Bolt Books Plant Experiment Series. Minneapolis, Minn.: Lerner Publishing Group, 2015.

Latham, Donna. *Respiration and Photosynthesis*. Sci-Hi: Life Science Series. Oxford, England: Raintree Publishers, 2016.

Maloof, Torrey. *Photosynthesis*. Science Readers: Content and Literacy Series. Huntington Beach, Calif.: Teacher Created Materials, 2015.

INTERNET SITES

Use Facthound to find Internet sites related to this book.

Visit *www.facthound.com*

Just type in 9781543529524 and go!

 Check out projects, games and lots more at
www.capstonekids.com

INDEX